IT'S THE EUCHARIST,
THANK GOD

First published in 2009 by Decani Books, Oak House, 70 High Street, Brandon Suffolk, IP27 0AU • http://www.decanimusic.co.uk

ISBN   978-1-900314-19-0

Printed by Quadrant Design and Print Solutions, Riverside House, Dicker Mill, Hertford, SG13 7AE

ACKNOWLEDGEMENT. We are grateful to the International Committee on English in the Liturgy for permission to quote from copyright texts (see pages 71-74 for full acknowledgement).

It's the Eucharist, thank God

Maurice Taylor

 Decani Books

Contents

Foreword

This is a book about the Eucharist. It is a miscellany, a collection of different items on the Mass: some theology of the 'Mystery of Faith'; a summary of how the liturgy has developed through the centuries; the liturgical reforms of the Second Vatican Council and their acceptance (or not); an account (by an insider) of the conflict that has marred the work of translating the Missal into English; and an outline of recent papal teaching on the Eucharist.

So much has been written on the Eucharist; so much could still be written and undoubtedly will be written. But I hope that this selection will prove helpful and interesting for 'ordinary people'. It aims to give an up-to-date appreciation of 'the source and summit of the Christian life' as well as a frank account of some of the controversial and painful issues that have arisen as a result of the liturgical renewal of Mass in the Roman rite.

I am grateful to Dr John R. Page, former Executive Secretary of ICEL, for checking the factual details of Sections 4 and 5. The opinions and judgments expressed are, however, mine.

Maurice Taylor

One
Introduction

IN THE CONTEMPORARY AND OFFICIAL TEACHING DOCUMENTS of the Church, there is a short description of the Eucharist. The wording comes from the Second Vatican Council's Constitution on the Sacred Liturgy, sometimes called *Sacrosanctum Concilium* (because these are the first words of the Latin text of the document), §47, which is repeated in the Catechism of the Catholic Church, §1323.

> At the Last Supper, on the night he was betrayed, our Saviour instituted the eucharistic sacrifice of his body and blood. This he did in order to perpetuate the sacrifice of the cross throughout the ages until he should come again, and so to entrust to his beloved spouse, the Church, a memorial of his death and resurrection, a sacrament of love, a sign of unity, a bond of charity, a paschal banquet in which Christ is consumed, the mind is filled with grace, and a pledge of future glory is given to us.

The Eucharist, which the Second Vatican Council calls 'the source and summit of the Christian life' (Dogmatic Constitution on the Church, *Lumen Gentium*, 11), should be celebrated with the active involvement of those present. In it they are nourished by the Lord's word and fed at the Lord's table:

> They should give thanks to God; by offering the immaculate victim not only through the hands of the priest but also with him, they should learn to offer themselves; through Christ their mediator, they should be drawn day by day into ever more perfect union with God and with each other, so that finally God may be all in all' (*Sacrosanctum Concilium* 48).

Essentially unchanged, indeed unchangeable; but in non-essentials

- presentation, style, appearance and involvement - greatly changed: that is the Mass following the 'reforms' of the Second Vatican Council in the 1960s. To be more accurate, it is the Mass in the Roman rite of the Latin Church.

Let me explain that last sentence. The Catholic (meaning 'world-wide') Church comprises several local or regional Churches, each with its own patriarch and all of them united in faith and moral teaching. All of them acknowledge the primacy and authority of the Bishop of Rome, the Pope. Each of these Churches has its own rite, that is, its way of celebrating the Eucharist and other sacred ceremonies.

Here we are concerned with the Latin Church, whose patriarch is the Pope. But in the Latin Church there are in fact several rites. All of them, except the Roman rite, are localised and not generally used in English-speaking nations. The Roman rite is much more widespread than any other rite in the Latin Church. It is this rite to which the overwhelming majority of Catholics belong and which is the subject of this book.

When the Second Vatican Council (1962-65) met, there is no doubt that one of its principal purposes was to renew and revise the Church's liturgy. The very first paragraph of the Council's Constitution on the Sacred Liturgy states:

> The sacred Council has set out to impart an ever-increasing vigour to the Christian life of the faithful; to adapt more closely to the needs of our age those institutions which are subject to change; to foster whatever can promote union among all who believe in Christ; to strengthen whatever can help to call all mankind into the Christian fold. Accordingly it sees particularly cogent reasons for the reform and promotion of the liturgy. (§1)

The Constitution defines that word 'liturgy' as follows:

> The liturgy, then, is rightly seen as an exercise of the priestly office of Jesus Christ. It involves the presentation of man's sanctification under the guise of signs perceptible by the

senses and its accomplishment in ways appropriate to each of these signs. In it, full public worship is performed by the Mystical Body of Jesus Christ, that is, by its Head and members. (§7)

Briefly, the intention of the Council was to impart to the liturgy 'new vigour to meet present-day circumstances and needs' (§4).

It is a principal aim of this book to consider how faithfully we nowadays, more than forty years on from the Second Vatican Council's teaching on the liturgy, observe that teaching and, specifically, its teaching on the Mass. How aware and how appreciative are we of what we should be doing when we gather in worship?

To achieve this aim we shall have to remind ourselves of some relevant theology ('What is the Mass?') and recall the teaching of the Council and the implications of that teaching ('How should we of the Roman rite celebrate Mass?'). Reaching correct responses to these two questions will enable us to make a reasonable attempt to judge how well the liturgy of the Mass is being celebrated.

Such a judgment will, of course, vary from place to place and from person to person. It will depend to a great extent on one's experience. My own experience is mainly in Scotland and specifically in the diocese of Galloway, but it is not limited to that. I hope that what I write will stimulate others to 'see, judge and act'. No participant at Mass should be merely a spectator or critic but should want to improve the way in which God is worshipped in the liturgy of the Church.

On a point of terminology, there are various names for our central act of worship. In English there are two common words: Mass and Eucharist. I shall use them interchangeably as I think normal contemporary usage does, even though the two words have different sources and histories. It should be clear also, that we are not using the word 'Eucharist' in the various restricted meanings that it sometimes has; as in, for example, 'receiving the Eucharist' and 'the sacrament of the Eucharist'. These uses are in contrast to 'the sacrifice of the Eucharist' or even 'the liturgy of the Eucharist' when distinguished from the Liturgy of the Word.

We should also note that, in addition to the sense in which we have already used the word 'rite', the same word is sometimes used to describe some parts of our liturgy, such as 'the opening rite', 'the Communion rite', 'the rite of blessing holy water' etc. The context will enable us to avoid the danger of confusion.

Two
'Mystery of Faith'

What are we doing at Mass?

JUST AFTER THE CONSECRATION OF THE BREAD AND WINE AT MASS, the priest proclaims to the participants these words: 'The Mystery of Faith'; or, if the Mass is in Latin, 'Mysterium Fidei'.

These are apt words to give us a hint of what we are doing. 'Mystery' because it is something that we cannot fully fathom; but something that indicates in symbols what it is; something that is expressed in signs, but signs that are what they signify, and not empty signs. 'Of faith' because it is revealed by God and given to us, to be believed and accepted gratefully and with certainty, guaranteed by the absolute truthfulness of God.

The phrase 'Mystery of Faith' of course takes us only a very little way towards knowing what the Mass is. It is possible for us to go further than simply saying that it is a mystery of faith, although a full explanation is beyond us.

On the night before his death, Jesus assembled his apostles in a room in Jerusalem and there had supper with them. During that meal he took some bread from the table, pronounced over it the words, 'This is my body', and then distributed it to the apostles, telling them to eat it. Then he took a cup of wine and, having said over it the words, 'This is my blood', he passed the cup round so that the apostles could drink from it. He added some other words: first, that his blood was the sign of a new and everlasting covenant between God and humankind; and second, that his blood would be shed for the forgiveness of the sins of the apostles and of others - great numbers of others. Significantly Jesus concluded by saying 'Do this in memory of me', a command which Christians have understood as applying not only to the apostles but to all who would follow them as disciples of Christ.

The Catholic Church believes that what took place at the Last Supper was truly sacrificial; not a distinct sacrifice from what was to take place the following day on Calvary but somehow, mysteriously, identified with it, anticipating it. How? We can only speculate. Perhaps by a divine ability to prescind from, or to overcome, the created restrictions of differences in time and location.

If there is a relationship of identity between the Last Supper and Calvary, and if Mass is the repetition of the Last Supper, the conclusion is that the relationship between Calvary and the Mass is also one of identity.

Admittedly, we cannot explain this identification but we maintain that it is achievable, and achieved, by God's power. We believe that the Last Supper and also every Mass are sacrificial because they are the saving work of Calvary, anticipated (in the case of the Last Supper) and renewed (in the case of Mass).

Sometimes Catholic theology describes the relationship between Calvary and Mass as a 're-presentation' of the former. The hyphen is important because, without it, we would be asserting that Mass is no more sacrificial (as it is less dramatic) than a passion play, merely a reminder or a depiction of Calvary.

We must also carefully avoid, when doing the theology of the Mass, the use of words that might suggest that the Mass is another sacrifice, a repetition of Calvary. That would indicate that Calvary was insufficient for our salvation or that it is not the one and only sacrifice which Jesus made. Christ does not sacrifice himself 'again'; even less does he suffer death 'again'.

Two other points may be made here. First, when Jesus and the apostles gathered for the Last Supper, something else happened. Only the gospel according to John mentions it but nevertheless it was highly significant then and it still is for us. The incident is that of Jesus washing the feet of the apostles. This was a powerful sign of our call to reach out to others and especially those in need. Later on, we shall see that, in recent documents, both Pope John Paul II and Pope Benedict XVI discuss this social mission and its importance for us more fully.

The other point that should be made is this. Nowadays, when the Church reflects on the saving work that Jesus carried out for us, we do not restrict our thoughts to our Lord's passion and death but we include also his rising from the tomb. The resurrection is seen as an integral part of the saving process and not merely the restoration of life to Jesus as a kind of reward for his redemptive suffering. Hence we see the Mass as a re-presentation of the complete saving work of our Lord; especially that the Jesus who is truly present in several ways when we celebrate Mass – including the holy communion that we receive – is the risen, living Christ and in no way a saviour who is dying again, even less a dead Christ.

The Mass in History

There are narratives describing the institution of the Eucharist at the Last Supper in the three synoptic gospels (Matthew, Mark and Luke). The earliest of all the New Testament narratives is to be found in St Paul's first letter to the Christians of Corinth. The oldest extant account of the liturgical celebration of the Eucharist by a Christian community is that given by St Justin the Martyr. It dates from around 155 AD.

> On the day we call the day of the sun, all who dwell in the city or the country gather in the same place. The memoirs of the apostles and the writings of the prophets are read as much as time permits. When the reader has finished, he who presides over those gathered admonishes and challenges them to imitate these beautiful things.
>
> Then we all rise together and offer prayers for ourselves… and for all others, wherever they may be, so that we may be found righteous by our life and actions, and faithful to the commandments, so as to obtain eternal salvation. When the

prayers are concluded, we exchange the kiss.

Then someone brings bread and a cup of water and wine mixed together to him who presides over the brethren. He takes them and offers praise and glory to the Father of the universe, through the name of the Son and of the Holy Spirit and for a considerable time he gives thanks that we have been judged worthy of these gifts. When he has concluded the prayers and thanksgivings, all present give voice to an acclamation by saying 'Amen'.

When he who presides has given thanks and the people have responded, those whom we call deacons give to those present the 'eucharisted' bread, wine and water and take them to those who are absent.

The essentials of Mass are present in that early account: celebration on Sunday – community which gathers – presiding bishop/priest – sacred readings – homily – general intercessions – greeting of peace – bread, wine and water brought to the presider – eucharistic prayer of thanksgiving – holy communion.

This basic rite of the Eucharist is still as we have it today. Additions have been made during the centuries and, for many hundreds of years, there have been set texts for various prayers, especially the prayers of the presiding bishop or priest and the eucharistic prayer itself.

In the Roman rite there was a reform and reordering of the Mass texts, imposed by Pope St Pius V in 1570. This is sometimes called the Tridentine rite, named for the Council of Trent (Concilium Tridentinum) which had decreed the reform a few years earlier.

Those sixteenth century texts were strictly enforced and observed until the reforms of the Second Vatican Council. That Council, in addition to permitting the use of the vernacular, also decreed a simplification of the texts and actions of the Tridentine rite. These were adjudged too complicated, too repetitive and, for the contemporary Church, a hindrance to the proper level of participation by those who are present. All of this is contained in the Council's Constitution on the Sacred Liturgy, *Sacramentum Concilium*, 4 December 1963. As a consequence, in 1969 Pope Paul VI issued the new Roman Missal.

The Council's decision to allow the use of the vernacular did not specify how much of the Mass could be celebrated in the vernacular: '…especially the readings and the 'common prayer' and also, as local conditions may warrant, in those parts which pertain to the people…' (§54). However, within a few years, the Holy See permitted the use of the local languages, properly approved and authorised, for all the texts of the Mass. Hence, the first edition in English of the Roman Missal was ready for publication in 1973 and on sale shortly afterwards.

More Theology of the Eucharist

The celebration of Mass unites us with the redemptive actions of Jesus, his death and resurrection. This redemptive work is often called the Paschal Mystery because it brings about the liberation of God's people from sin and death. The adjective 'paschal' is from the noun 'Pasch' which refers to God's liberation of the Israelites from Egypt. Freed by God's 'passing over' his people and the destroying angel sparing the first-born sons of those Israelites where the doorpost was smeared with the blood of a paschal lamb, God's people made their Exodus from slavery and began their journey to the Promised Land.

That Exodus was – and still is – solemnly commemorated each year by Jews at the paschal supper. It was at such a meal, the meal we call 'the Last Supper', that Jesus not only instituted our Eucharist but also related it to the Jewish Passover as the latter's definitive and complete fulfilment. In consequence of this, Christ's redemptive work, his death and resurrection on Calvary or when made sacramentally present at the Last Supper and also at Mass, is known as his paschal mystery.

There is another powerful link between the Mass and the earlier history of the relationship between God and his people. This lies in the fact that Jesus, at the Last Supper, spoke of his blood, shed for us, as the sign of the new and eternal covenant between God and humankind.

A covenant is a pledged agreement of total mutual fidelity, made between two parties; in the religious sense, it is made between God and humans. In the Old Testament, God made such a covenant several times with his people; specifically, the covenant, inaugurated with Moses on Mount Sinai during the Exodus journey, was renewed on several occasions, especially when Israel had proved unfaithful and God was recalling his people to his plan of salvation for them: 'I will be your God and you shall be my people'. And this pact was sealed and ratified by the sacrifice of an animal and the shedding of its blood.

In the New Testament, all four accounts of the Last Supper which describe our Lord's consecration of bread and wine attach covenant language to the consecration of the latter.

The shortest formula is preserved by Mark:

> This is my blood, the blood of the covenant, which will be shed for many (Mk 14:24).

Matthew adds: 'for the remission of sins' (Mt 26:28). Luke and Paul have: 'This cup is the new covenant in my blood' (Lk 22:20; 1Cor 11:25) and Luke alone: 'which is going to be shed for you' (Lk 22:20). The passing of the cup is a ritual gesture. The words pronounced bind it to the act which Jesus is on the point of accomplishing: his death, accepted freely for the redemption of many.

> ... 'the blood of the covenant' recalls also that the covenant of Sinai had been concluded in blood (Exod 24:8); for the sacrifices of animals, there was substituted a new sacrifice, the blood of which would efficaciously achieve a definitive union between God and men... And because this act will henceforth be rendered present in a ritual gesture which Jesus commanded to "do again in memory of him" it is by the eucharistic participation, accomplished by faith, that the faithful will be united most intimately to the mystery of the new covenant and that they will benefit from its graces.

[Xavier Léon-Dufour ed., *Dictionary of Biblical Theology*, art. *Covenant*, p.97]

Our celebration of, and participation in, Mass is thus our opportunity consciously to renew our side of the sacred covenant with God, dedicating ourselves once again to belong to God, to be faithful to God through the graces won for us by Jesus Christ, our Saviour. To receive holy communion from the chalice is an opportunity which should not be missed to express openly and indeed dramatically our desire to engage ourselves as God's covenanted people.

———

There is a further dimension of the Eucharist that is sometimes overlooked. Already we have seen that the Eucharist makes present to us the saving work of Jesus, his death and resurrection. Moreover, the celebration of Mass not merely reminds us of its roots in Israel's history but can truly be said to be a development of that history; indeed, derived directly from it, continuing it and bringing it to its fullness in Christ.

So the Mass looks back. But it also looks forward to the parousia, the second coming of Christ in glory, the end of the world as we know it, eternal life. At the Last Supper, our Lord declared that he 'would not drink again of the fruit of the vine until the Kingdom of God comes' (Lk 22:18), thus making a connection between the Eucharist and the end time. But the connection, the eschatological dimension of the Eucharist as it is called, is much more clearly expressed in the texts that occur in every Mass. This is especially so in the eucharistic prayer and perhaps above all in the memorial acclamations which nowadays follow the consecration of the bread and wine. Hence,

'...we proclaim your death, O Lord, until you come again'.

The Eucharist in thus looking forward to eternal life is often described as the pledge of future glory; just as that future glory, being the fulfilment of the Eucharist, is called the banquet of the Paschal Lamb.

We shall return to this in Section Six, as also to some frequently neglected implications of our taking part in Mass; namely, that we are ourselves henceforward committed to proclaiming and sharing our faith with others and to showing our loving concern for those in need. Both John Paul II (in his Apostolic Letter *Mane Nobiscum Domine*) and Benedict XVI (in the Apostolic Exhortation *Sacramentum Caritatis*) stress these aspects of eucharistic faith and practice.

———

To conclude these observations on the theology of the Mass we can remind ourselves of the description (already quoted above, in the Introduction) of the Mass found in the Constitution on the Sacred Liturgy (*Sacrosanctum Concilium*) of the Second Vatican Council.

> At the Last Supper, on the night he was betrayed, our Saviour instituted the eucharistic sacrifice of his body and blood. This he did in order to perpetuate the sacrifice of the cross throughout the ages until he should come again, and so to entrust to his beloved spouse, the Church, a memorial of his death and resurrection, a sacrament of love, a sign of unity, a bond of charity, a paschal banquet in which Christ is consumed, the mind is filled with grace, and a pledge of future glory is given to us. (§47)

The Catechism of the Catholic Church repeats the words of the Council. The Compendium of the Catechism, issued in 2006, some twelve years after the Catechism, follows the Council's teaching closely but manages to avoid that breathlessly long sentence.

> The Eucharist is the very sacrifice of the Body and Blood of the Lord Jesus which he instituted to perpetuate the sacrifice of the cross throughout the ages until his return in glory. Thus he entrusted to his Church this memorial of his death and resurrection. It is a sign of unity, a bond of charity, a paschal banquet, in which Christ is consumed, the mind is filled with grace, and a pledge of future glory is given to us. (§271)

Many of the phrases of these definitions go back to the short antiphon, composed in the thirteenth century, probably by St Thomas Aquinas, for use in the liturgical festivities of the newly instituted feast of the Eucharist, Corpus Christi.

> O sacrum convivium,
> In quo Christus sumitur,
> Passio eius recolitur,
> Mens impletur gratiae,
> Et futurae gloriae nobis pignus datur.

(see page 103 for an English translation.)

Three
The Old or the New? Trent v. Vatican II

IT MAY SEEM STRANGE THAT ACTIONS AND TEXTS OF MASS in the Roman rite which had served the Church well for four hundred years should have been subject to so much change as a result of the Second Vatican Council. In its opening paragraphs the Constitution on the Liturgy speaks of its aim 'to adapt more closely to the needs of our age those institutions which are subject to change' (§1) and of its desire 'that, where necessary, the rites be revised carefully in the light of sound tradition and that they be given new vigour ro meet present day circumstances and needs' (§4).

Later, the Council spoke much more trenchantly.

> In order that the Christian people may more certainly derive an abundance of graces from the sacred liturgy, holy Mother Church desires to undertake with great care a general restoration of the liturgy itself. For the liturgy is made up of unchangeable elements divinely instituted and of elements subject to change. These latter not only may be changed but also ought to be changed with the passage of time, if they have suffered from the intrusion of anything out of harmony with the inner nature of the liturgy or have become less suitable. In this restoration, both texts and rites should be drawn up so as to express more clearly the holy things that they signify. The Christian people, as far as is possible, should be able to understand them with ease and take part in them fully, actively and as a community. (§21)

The Constitution goes on to list a series of principles that should govern such 'restoration'. Then, coming to the chapter specifically on the Eucharist, the document teaches:

The Church, therefore, earnestly desires that Christ's faithful, when present at this mystery of faith, should not be there as strangers or silent spectators. On the contrary, through a good understanding of the rites and prayers they should take part in the sacred action, conscious of what they are doing, with devotion and full collaboration. (§48)

For this reason the sacred Council, having in mind those Masses which are celebrated with the faithful assisting, especially on Sundays and holidays of obligation, has made the following decrees so that the sacrifice of the Mass, even in the ritual forms [of the celebration], may have full pastoral efficacy. (§49)

The rite of the Mass is to be revised in such a way that the intrinsic nature and purpose of its several parts, as well as the connection between them, may be more clearly manifested, and that devout and active participation by the faithful may be more easily achieved.

For this purpose, the rites are to be simplified, due care being taken to preserve their substance. Parts which with the passage of time came to be duplicated, or were added with little advantage, are to be omitted. Other parts which suffered loss through accidents of history are to be restored to the vigour they had in the days of the holy Fathers, as may seem useful or necessary. (§50)

These are far-reaching instructions, calling for quite dramatic alterations in the way that the liturgy, and in particular the Eucharist, is celebrated in the Roman rite. The fundamental aim is that those present at Mass should be genuinely participating and in a manner that is intelligent, active and devout.

The Tridentine Mass

Over the years since these decisions of the Second Vatican Council, the Mass in the pre-conciliar rite has survived and still continues to be celebrated. This situation has been occasioned by those who are unhappy with the Vatican II liturgy (sometimes called the Mass of Paul VI since it was promulgated and introduced by him). Such unhappiness has been of varying intensity. At its most vehement, there are those who reject the Mass of Paul VI completely on grounds that it is not a valid celebration of the Eucharist.

One recognises the pastoral concern of the Holy See to heal or avoid such actual or possible schism in the Church. Moreover, there are others who, while admitting the validity of the Mass of Paul VI, are unhappy with it and who prefer, or claim to prefer, Mass according to the pre-conciliar rite.

In an effort to please the dissatisfied, permission to use the pre-conciliar rite has been slowly and gradually extended by the Holy See, notably by Pope John Paul II in 1984 and 1988. This process culminated on 29 June 2007 with Benedict XVI's *Motu Proprio*, entitled (from the first two words of the Latin original) *Summorum Pontificum*.

The *Motu Proprio* gives much wider scope for the use of the pre-Vatican II form of Mass for those who wish to celebrate the Eucharist in that way. Bishops are still authorised to regulate its practice; however, if the local bishop is unable or unwilling to accede to requests from a group of lay faithful, the matter is to be referred ro the Holy See for consideration of their wish and for help in achieving it.

There is considerable debate about *Summorum Pontificum*. Does it not abrogate the intention, if not the explicit decision, of the Second Vatican Council that the earlier form of Mass should be superseded? Does it not remove from bishops their lawful authority to decide when they will permit limited use of the earlier Missal? Will it not lead to division and confusion in parishes and/or dioceses?

An improvement?

Another area of debate is concerned with the relative values of the two forms of the rite of Mass. Is the newer, post-Vatican II form an improvement on the earlier form? Did we lose something of importance when the earlier form was (or was thought to be) superseded?

There can, of course, be no suggestion that either form is somehow invalid. However, is there something to be said for the retention of the older form, something valuable that has been lost in the new Missal, something so valuable that it has to be retained as arguably a perfectly acceptable alternative way of celebrating Mass in the Roman rite? And, if so, did *Sacrosanctum Concilium* merely offer an alternative without the intention of its replacing the previous form?

In his Motu Proprio, Pope Benedict repeats what all earlier permissions to use the pre-Vatican II rite of Mass required: that those celebrating in this way must nonetheless fully accept the validity and legitimacy of the Paul VI rite of Mass. Pope Benedict avoids the terms 'Tridentine rite' or 'Mass of Pius V' for the pre-Vatican II rite, preferring to name it 'the Mass of John XXIII' since the final edition of the Missal in question (with a few minor alterations from previous editions) occurred in 1962 during the pontificate of John XXIII and just before the start of the Second Vatican Council. Pope Benedict also uses the term 'the ordinary form of the Roman rite' for the post-Vatican II liturgy, the earlier being 'the extraordinary form'.

Let us return to *Sacrosanctum Concilium* and recall the reasons it adduced for ordering a revision and reform of the rite and texts of the Mass.

It spoke of 'adaptations to the needs of our times' and 'careful revision to meet today's needs and circumstances'. The revision would make the rites more easily understood and would foster full, active and communal participation and provide 'an abundance of graces' for the Christian people. The Council wanted the reforms in order that conscious, active and full participation would enable liturgical celebration to have its 'full pastoral efficacy' (§§1, 4, 21, 48 & 49). The clear implication of this is that the pre-Vatican II rite (the Mass of John XXIII, aka 'the extraordinary form of the Roman rite') did not fulfil the Council's criteria for 'full pastoral efficacy'. Why did it not?

Before we try to answer that question, however, we must avoid the assumption that our post-Vatican II Mass precludes the use of

Latin or that, when celebrating it, the priest must face the congregation. The 'ordinary form' may be celebrated in Latin and with the celebrant having his back to the people. Hence, calls to restore Mass in Latin or to have the priest 'facing the wall' are not arguments for a return of the Mass of John XXIII. Nor is it correct to argue that abuses or lack of reverence which sometimes occur in the celebration of the ordinary form demand the return of the extraordinary form; the remedy for any abuses or irreverence lies in a stricter vigilance over the ordinary form of Mass.

On the other hand, when the older rite is celebrated, it has to be in Latin. How many priests can do that? How many people can understand the language? Even more basically, are the strong pastoral arguments of the Pope and all the bishops of the Church at the Second Vatican Council for a revision of the rite of Mass mistaken or, at least, unconvincing?

The Mass of John XXIII examined

The form in which Mass had to be celebrated was laid down by Pope Pius V in 1570 (the so-called Tridentine Mass). Since Missals with this form were published, as we have seen, until 1962, Pope Benedict XVI has now called this celebration of the liturgy 'the Mass of John XXIII' or 'Mass in the extraordinary form of the Roman rite'.

This form of Mass has, of course, to be celebrated in Latin, with no concelebration allowed, no holy communion under both kinds, no reception of the host in the hand. In this 'extraordinary form', there is no separation between the altar of sacrifice, the ambo for the Scripture readings and the chair of the presiding priest. The readings take place at the altar.

Introductory Rites

'The Mass of John XXIII' begins 'at the foot of the altar steps'. A Latin dialogue takes place between priest and male server(s), comprising the forty-second psalm, the Confiteor (said first by the priest and then repeated by the server) and a further short exchange of verses and responses between priest and server. (All of this is partly omitted and partly changed in 'the ordinary form of the Roman rite', i.e., the post-Vatican II form, because it originated as the priest's private preparation for Mass as he approached the altar).

The priest then ascends the steps and, at the altar, says the Introit (an entry antiphon), the Kyrie and, on Sundays and feast days, the Gloria. (These are retained in our ordinary form but with adaptations to bring a more meaningful arrangement to them and to enable the people to participate). The Opening Prayers (Collects) are often the same in both ordinary and extraordinary forms, although there have been changes in the texts of some of the prayers and there is now a single opening prayer where, previously, there could be several, one following another. Further, in the ordinary form, the priest is at the chair, not at the altar, for these parts of Mass.

The Scripture Readings

The Scripture readings in the two forms of the Roman rite differ considerably. In the older form there is a very limited selection, little or no sequence in the readings, either from the gospels or from other parts of the Bible (the 'semi-continuous readings') from Sunday to Sunday or from weekday to weekday. The Old Testament is hardly present in the extraordinary form, lay readers and cantors are not used, and the responsorial psalm exists only in embryonic form. The Liturgy of the Word in the earlier form is carried out, in Latin, by the priest at the altar and, presumably, facing away from the people to whom he is reading. It is true that the priest can interrupt his celebration at this point in order to go to a pulpit to read the epistle and gospel in the vernacular, to make announcements and to give a sermon (not necessarily a homily to 'open' the readings or other parts of the Mass for the benefit of the faithful).

It seems to me that the interlude at the pulpit only serves to underline the inadequacy of the way in which the Liturgy of the Word is celebrated in the older, extraordinary form of the Roman rite.

When Mass in the extraordinary form is resumed with the priest back at the altar, the Creed, if to be said, is recited by the priest alone and in Latin. There may be a choir to sing the Credo; in that case, the priest has still to recite the profession of faith 'into himself' and then leave the altar to sit down at the side of the sanctuary to wait until the choir has finished. (A similar procedure occurs if there is a choir to sing a Gloria.) Our present general intercessions (i.e., the 'bidding prayers'), recovered from the early centuries of the Church, simply do not happen in the extraordinary form of Mass.

The Liturgy of the Eucharist

The next section of the liturgy, once called the Offertory and now called the Preparation of the Gifts, is more altered in the ordinary form and more simplified than any other section of the extraordinary form. In the latter, the priest's words, said silently, could easily give the impression that it is the bread and wine that are being offered in sacrifice. The following, for example, are the words (in English) which the priest says in Latin in what is called 'The Offering of the Host'.

> Receive, O Holy Father, almighty and eternal God, this spotless host which I, Thine unworthy servant, offer unto Thee, my living and true God, for my countless sins, trespasses, and omissions; likewise for all here present, and for all faithful Christians, whether living or dead, that it may avail both me and them to salvation, unto everlasting life. Amen.

Rather than the sentiments of that prayer, the truth is that the gifts are merely being set aside or dedicated because, in the eucharistic prayer, they will be changed into the body and blood of Christ; then, and only then, the sacrificial offering to the Father takes place. For this reason, this earlier part of Mass should no longer be called the Offertory. In the ordinary form, the gifts can be brought to the priest by members of the congregation to symbolise their involvement; and the prayers said by the priest as he dedicates the bread and wine are modelled upon dedicatory prayers used in Jewish worship (as Jesus would have done at the Last Supper). This section of Mass in the ordinary form ends with the second prayer of the presiding priest, the Prayer over the Gifts (more recently, the Prayer over the Offerings), said aloud and in the plural in the name of all present. In the extraordinary form of Mass, the prayer is known as the 'Secret'; it is said inaudibly by the priest despite the prayer being in the plural and on behalf of the people.

I have already mentioned the unsuitability of treating the bread and wine as if they were the sacrifice being offered to God. The older Missal also prescribes a number of movements and gestures to be performed by the priest in an attempt to embellish and add solemnity to the liturgy but which, nowadays, seem to many to be merely repetitive, fussy and exaggerated.

The Eucharistic Prayer

The eucharistic prayer in the pre-Vatican II form is retained in the post-conciliar form and is known as Eucharistic Prayer I or the Roman Canon. It is unchanged, except that a memorial acclamation is now inserted after the institution narrative and the elevation of the host and chalice. The whole congregation is asked to join in this acclamation as well as the other two which already were in the Roman Canon: the Holy, Holy (Sanctus) and the final Great Amen. However, the gestures required of the priest are simplified in the ordinary form of the rite; in particular, the number of blessings (signs of the cross) which the priest repeatedly made over the bread and wine, ten before and fifteen after their consecration - a number surely bordering on the ridiculous - are now greatly reduced – in fact, to one.

In addition to the retention of the Roman Canon in the ordinary form of the Roman rite, several other eucharistic prayers (and many new prefaces) are to be found alongside it: Eucharistic Prayers II, III and IV; three Eucharistic Prayers for Masses with Children; two for Masses of Reconciliation; and four forms of a Eucharistic Prayer for Various Needs and Occasions.

Each one of these extra post-Vatican II eucharistic prayers follows the same orderly structure: introductory dialogue, preface and acclamation, address of worship to God, epiclesis (invoking the Holy Spirit to come so that the elements may be consecrated into Christ's body and blood), institution narrative, elevation and acclamation, anamnesis (relating the Mass to Calvary) and offering of our sacrifice to the Father, prayer that those taking part may be filled with the Spirit, invocation of the saints, prayer for the living and the dead, solemn doxology and final acclamation.

As one admires this orderly sequence, it has to be admitted that the Roman Canon, though venerable, does not have such a clear structure. Since it was assembled gradually, with extra parts added in the course of time, it tends to be disorganised with duplication of the intercessory elements and the invocation of the saints, a certain amount of repetition and, perhaps its greatest lack, the absence of an explicit epiclesis.

However, I think that, because it was so familiar, most people appreciate that it 'survived' the Council's reform of the liturgy, especially as we were given so many extra eucharistic prayers for our alternative use. Any attempt to reconstruct the Roman Canon would probably have failed. The question can legitimately be asked: since the Roman Canon was retained, does that not imply that the other parts of the pre-Council liturgy, those which were not retained, were presumed to be suppressed in favour of the reformed texts (rather than, as now, resuscitated and offered as alternatives)?

Communion

The communion rite follows the eucharistic prayer. It begins with the Lord's Prayer and ends with the third of the presider's prayers. This latter is sometimes called the post-communion prayer. The rite as it was before the Council has been largely retained, with one notable addition and an important modification.

The addition is an extension of the rite of peace. Where previously the priest gave a greeting to all ('*Pax Domini sit semper vobiscum*') to which the server alone (despite '*vobiscum*', a plural form) responded, now there is a prayer, said aloud by the priest, asking Our Lord for peace among us, for the Church and for the world. Then comes the greeting to which the whole congregation responds before the people are invited to exchange a sign of peace with those who are nearby.

The modification is a new emphasis that the members of the congregation will share in receiving holy communion. Previously, the rite seemed to indicate a concentration only on the priest's communion (silent prayers, the chalice for him alone). Holy communion for the faithful, if not quite an afterthought, was nonetheless an appendage. Indeed, holy communion for the people was sometimes begun by a priest, not the celebrant, soon after the consecration, or delayed until Mass was over, or did not happen at all; and, when it did, the chalice was never an option. I recall also the bizarre teaching, before the Council, that, to avoid the mortal sin of missing Mass on Sundays, one need only be present for the offertory, the consecration and the priest's communion.

In the ordinary form of Mass, a period of silence is recommended when holy communion is over and before the priest says the Prayer after Communion. It has to be admitted that this silence, not envisaged in the extraordinary form, is often very compressed in the ordinary form.

Concluding Rite

The concluding rite of Mass in the ordinary form is brief, simple and direct: a blessing for the people and their dismissal. This latter is not meant as 'You are free to go now' but 'Go into the world outside to proclaim your faith'.

The additions which had crept into the pre-conciliar Mass, especially the so-called Last Gospel (the first verses of St John's gospel) are omitted in the ordinary form. They were originally a private prayer of the priest as he left the sanctuary. They make little sense as an element in the liturgy, especially as the people have already been dismissed (or so they thought!)

The two forms: preferences and comparisons

I think that it is a pity that there has been an increased permission, even encouragement, to restore the use in the Roman rite of the 'extraordinary form', i.e., the Tridentine rite, the rite of Pius V and John XXIII. The comparison of the two forms, ordinary and extraordinary, leaves little doubt of the great improvements achieved as a result of the reforms and revision ordered by the Second Vatican Council. The liturgy of Mass is now clear, intelligible for all and participative.

Those who prefer the extraordinary form give various reasons: it is in Latin, it provides an atmosphere of awe and mystery, it generates respect and prayerfulness etc. However, and in reply to these arguments: Latin can be used for the ordinary form of the rite; and the desire for a sense of mystery suggests that some people would welcome a screen to separate priest from people and hide the former (as in the Orthodox liturgy). If admittedly, we do not have an atmosphere of sufficient silence, reverence and respect when Mass is celebrated in the ordinary form, that is not a problem intrinsic to the ordinary form. If there is a fault here, it can be remedied by our behaviour, by education and awareness, without the need to throw out the baby with the bath water.

• Music

It is often said that the music associated with the post-conciliar missal is banal, trite and impoverished. This may well be true in some cases and to an extent, but it is not the fault of the ordinary form of the rite. Following the strong encouragement in the Constitution on the Liturgy, the ordinary rite welcomes good sacred music and it is the duty of dioceses and parishes to foster and use it.

However, there are certain conditions that have to be kept in mind. First, it should be parts of the Mass that are sung, and not primarily hymns, even suitably chosen and appropriate to the Mass of the day. Second, the music should not be the monopoly of a choir but should allow at least some participation by the congregation. Third, those parts of the Mass which are better sung than said, especially the Gloria, Sanctus and Agnus Dei, should not be mere paraphrases of the prescribed texts and should not be so extended that they interrupt the flow of the liturgical celebration.

These conditions, especially the second and third, are most frequently infringed at what we called Solemn High Mass in the extraordinary form. The priest, deacon and subdeacon had usually to leave the altar and go to sit down because the music for a particular section was so protracted and elaborate; and because of the character of the music, the congregation had no opportunity to participate. Papal Masses in St Peter's Basilica in Rome are outstanding examples of this – beautiful music, but the congregation is not involved in a way that allows proper participation.

• Rubrics

There is another aspect of Solemn High Masses in the extraordinary form that is intriguing. The rubrics speak of a celebrant (bishop or priest), deacon and subdeacon.

But the part of the deacon is usually taken by a priest (or, in papal Masses, even a cardinal!) which is a liturgical anomaly since people are supposed to take part according to the rank or order which they possess and not posing to be something else; further, the order of subdeacon no longer exists in the Latin church!

Besides all this, the rubrics of Solemn High Mass according to the extraordinary form call for a multiplicity of bowing to one another by those in the sanctuary and of kissing of hands and objects as the latter are handed to the celebrant (biretta, paten, chalice, thurible, even the little spoon for adding incense to the charcoal in the thurible). These actions are copied from the royal and ducal courts of baroque Europe; they are an embarrassing anachronism that ought to have no place in the Church's celebration of the Eucharist.

• 'Actively engaged'

As we know, the Church declares that the faithful are to be 'actively engaged' in the liturgy and wants those present at Mass to be there not

> as silent spectators; on the contrary, through an adequate understanding of the rites and prayers, they should take part in the sacred action conscious of what they are doing, with devotion and full collaboration.
>
> (*Sacrosanctum Concilium*, §11 and §48).

Surely, then, a cogent reason for the introduction of the new rite was that the old rite could not adequately provide these requirements. I suggest that here we have a case in which Christ's teaching has to be relevant: 'Nobody puts new wine into old wineskins; if he does, the wine will burst the skins and the wine is lost and the skins too. No! New wine, fresh skins!' (Mk 2:22).

Postscript

An interesting postscript to all of this is provided by some observations which Pope Benedict XVI made about *Summorum Pontificum* in September 2008. He was reported as saying:

> This *Motu Proprio* is simply an act of tolerance, with a pastoral objective, for people who have been formed in this liturgy, who love it, who know it, who want to live with this liturgy. It is a small group, because it supposes an education in Latin, a formation in a certain type of culture. But It seems to me a normal requirement of faith and pastoral practice for a bishop of our Church to have love and forbearance for these people and allow them to live with this liturgy.'

The implications of the Pope's words about the purpose of the *Motu Proprio* seem to me to be very significant indeed.

Four
Translating the Missal

English in the Liturgy

• The Lectionary

THE SECOND VATICAN COUNCIL OPENED THE WAY for the use of vernacular languages in the Roman rite, specifically in the 'ordinary form' of the liturgy. So far, we have said little on this subject, but it is time now to consider the matter in detail.

It is important to make a distinction straight away and to deal separately with the Scripture readings first and only later with the other liturgical texts.

The list of Scripture texts to be used in what is now called the ordinary form of the Roman rite was issued by the Holy See on Pentecost Sunday, 25 May 1969. It indicates the readings for Masses on Sundays, ordinary weekdays, feasts and special seasons. Since all the readings, including the psalms and gospel acclamations, were to be in the local languages, the Holy See decreed that local bishops' conferences should determine which translations would be used:

> The Constitution on the Sacred Liturgy directed that the treasures of the Bible be opened up more lavishly so that a richer share might be provided for the faithful at the table of God's word and a more representative portion of sacred Scripture be read to the people over a prescribed number of years (§ 51). In response to these directives, the Consilium for the Implementation of the Constitution on the Liturgy prepared this Lectionary for Mass and Pope Paul VI approved it in the apostolic constitution *Missale Romanum*, 3 April 1969...

...Since the *editio typica* of the New Order of Readings provides only text references, it is the responsibility of the conferences of bishops to prepare the complete vernacular texts, following the guidelines in the instruction on translation of liturgical texts (Consilium for the Implementation of the Constitution on the Liturgy, 25 January 1969). Vernacular texts may be taken from Bible translations already canonically approved for individual regions, with the confirmation of the Apostolic See. If newly translated, they should be submitted for confirmation to this Congregation.

(Decree of the Sacred Congregation for Divine Worship, 25 May 1969)

The bishops' conferences of England and Wales, Ireland, and Scotland chose and approved two versions of the Scriptures for use at Mass. These were the Revised Standard Version and the Jerusalem Bible with, in each case, the responsorial psalms taken from the Grail Psalter. Both versions of the lectionary, approved by the bishops' conferences and confirmed by the Holy See, were published, the choice of which to use being left to each parish. In the event, the great majority of parishes use the Jerusalem Bible. A revised edition of the lectionary, with a few additions and emendations, has been in use since 1981.

In the early years of the present century, the bishops' conferences of a number of English-speaking nations severally felt the need of a newly revised lectionary. This would not only contain all the additions and changes made by the Holy See since 1981, but would also use, as far as possible, the best up-to-date translation in the light of contemporary biblical scholarship.

The decision, for England and Wales, Ireland, and Scotland, was that the new lectionary in English for the twenty-first century would principally use the translation known as the New Revised Standard Version. The psalms, however, will continue to be the translations found in the Grail Psalter. The work necessary for the preparation and publication of the new lectionary (including issues of copyright and of inclusive language) has now begun, under the direction of an international commission drawn from a number of English-speaking countries. The commission's task, of course, is not to translate the passages to be used (as ICEL has to do) since it is dealing with the Scriptures, which are already in English.

• The Missal

In the Constitution on the Sacred Liturgy, the Second Vatican Council authorised, under certain conditions, the use of the vernacular languages in place of Latin in the Mass.

> A suitable place may be allotted to the vernacular in Masses which are celebrated with the people, especially in the readings and 'the common prayer' [the general intercessions] and also, as local conditions may warrant, in those parts which pertain to the people, according to the rules laid down in article 36 of this Constitution.
>
> Nevertheless, care must be taken to ensure that the faithful may also be able to say or sing together in Latin those parts of the Ordinary of the Mass which pertain to them.
>
> Whenever a more extended use of the vernacular in the Mass seems desirable, the regulation laid down in article 49 of this Constitution is to be observed. (§54)

The teaching in article 36 states:-

> (1) The use of the Latin language...is to be preserved in the Latin rite.
>
> (2)...Since the use of the vernacular...may frequently be of great advantage to the people, a wider use may be made of it, especially in readings, directives and in some prayers and chants. Regulations governing this will be given separately in subsequent chapters.
>
> (3) These norms being observed, it is for the competent territorial ecclesiastical authority mentioned in article 22:2 to decide whether, and to what extent, the vernacular language is to be used. Its decrees have to be approved, that is, confirmed, by the Apostolic See.

(4) Translations from the Latin for use in the liturgy must be approved by the competent territorial ecclesiastical authority already mentioned.

Article 22:2 reads as follows:-

In virtue of power conceded by law, the regulation of the liturgy within certain defined limits belongs also to certain kinds of bishops' conferences, legitimately established, with competence in given territories.

The wording of article 49 gives the reason for these provisions:-

For this reason, the sacred Council, having in mind those Masses which are celebrated with the faithful assisting, especially on Sundays and holidays of obligation, has made the following decrees so that the sacrifice of the Mass, even in the ritual form of its celebration, may have full pastoral efficacy.

From all of this, it is clear that the Council granted some use of the local languages in some parts of the Mass, as well as anticipating that, in due course, permission might well be extended to other parts of the Mass. That is what happened. Not only did such extension occur very quickly, within a few years of the Council, but in fact the local languages were authorised for the entire text of the Mass (and of other liturgies). Some provisional texts in English were rapidly issued and the complete Roman Missal in English was ready in 1973 and authorised, printed and published by 1974.

The birth of ICEL

The words from *Sacrosanctum Concilium* quoted above include an important practical guideline:

Where circumstances warrant it, it [the competent territorial ecclesiastical authority] is to consult with bishops of neighbouring regions which have the same language. (§36:3)

The Constitution on the Sacred Liturgy was formally passed and adopted by an overwhelming majority of the Council on 3 December 1963. Already, however, from the start of the Council the previous year, a number of English-speaking bishops from various nations had, with foresight, seen the need of some sort of international committee to enable English-speaking bishops' conferences to work together on the renewal of the liturgy and especially on producing worthy English translations of whatever liturgical texts the Council would authorise to be in the vernacular languages.

These bishops continued to plan for the future and, on 17 October 1963, an important meeting took place in the Venerable English College in Rome. Representatives of ten English-speaking bishops' conferences attended – Australia, Canada, England and Wales, India, Ireland, Pakistan, Scotland, Southern Africa and United States of America – and formally constituted ICEL, the International Commission on English in the Liturgy. Soon after ICEL came into existence, the Philippines bccame the eleventh member.

In addition, fifteen other bishops' conferences which required English texts became associate members of ICEL. These conferences, which were kept informed of developments by ICEL, are the Antilles (West Indies), Bangladesh, CEPAC (Pacific Islands), Gambia-Liberia-Sierra Leone, Ghana, Kenya, Malaysia-Singapore, Malawi, Nigeria, Papua New Guinea and the Solomons, Sri Lanka, Tanzania, Uganda. Zambia, Zimbabwe.

The International Commission was given its constitution, its structures and its method of working by the conferences which had established it.

The basic work in ICEL was done by teams of experts in various disciplines. These were charged with the responsibility of producing translations that would be faithful to the Latin original - but not so literal as to be stilted - and suitable for proclamation and for public prayer.

The translators' work was examined and, if necessary, revised by an Advisory Committee, the members of which, drawn from English-speaking countries sll over the world, were variously skilled in liturgy and sacramental theology, Scripture, Greek and Latin, English literature and music. The Advisory Committee had been established in 1964 in these deliberately explicit terms:-

'The Hierarchies of England and Wales, Scotland, Ireland, the United States of America, Canada, Australia, New Zealand, India, Pakistan, and Southern Africa, having agreed to the establishment of an International Advisory Committee on English in the Liturgy with a view to achieving an English version of liturgical texts acceptable to English-speaking countries and bearing in mind the ecumenical aspects, entrust the Committee with the following Mandate:

To work out a plan for the translation of liturgical texts and the provision of original texts where required in language which would be correct, dignified, intelligible and suitable for recitation and singing…'

The wording of this Mandate is worthy of note. In welcoming the skills and cooperation of those not in episcopal orders, the bishops were reflecting and following the experience of the Vatican Council itself, at which the Council bishops were glad to have the participation and advice of their *periti* (experts) in the preparation of the conciliar documents.

When the Advisory Committee of ICEL had completed its work on a liturgical text, the result was passed to the Episcopal Board. This Board, to which the member conferences had already given the direction of ICEL, comprised eleven members, one bishop from each of the bishops' conferences which were full members of the International Commission.

Once the Episcopal Board had approved texts, they were sent to the bishops' conferences. Each conference would be able to arrange a canonical vote to give formal approval (for which, a two-thirds majority was required); formal rejection was also an option for a conference. At last, the conference, when satisfied, would send the document to the Congregation for Divine Worship and the Discipline of the Sacraments (the current name of that dicastery) seeking confirmation (*recognitio*). When this had been obtained, the text could be published for use in that particular country.

That summarises the process, but it was a process that demanded and received meticulous attention from many experts and authorities. There were innumerable discussions and debates as well as the admission of amendments and alternative translations – a long, careful and demanding process.

The ICEL missal of 1974

The documents which ICEL translated comprised the rites of all the sacraments, the various liturgical books (RCIA, reconciliation, care of the sick, funerals…) but, of course, the principal texts, and those which concern us here, were those of the *Missale Romanum*. This contained the unchanging Order of Mass, prefaces, eucharistic prayers, and the three presidential prayers of each Mass for Sundays, feasts, commons, seasons, votive Masses – an enormous collection of more than 2000 texts.

Work on the translation of the Roman Missal proceeded very quickly in spite of the quantity of texts and the complicated nature of the work. The translation was complete in 1972. All the eleven bishops' conferences who are full members of ICEL approved it and the Holy See gave it the required confirmation (*recognitio*). Printing began in 1973 and, as already noted, the Missal was published in full for Great Britain and Ireland in the autumn of 1974.

This is the translation which we have been using ever since then, although there have been additions – new saints, some new eucharistic prayers (three for Masses with children, two for Masses of reconciliation, and four variants of a basic text for 'Masses for Various Needs and Occasions').

That missal has stood the test of time but it is not perfect. The translation, though done with care, was carried out with some urgency in order to have the English texts available as soon as possible. There are some inaccuracies and other occasions where the translation lacks felicity of expression. In particular, there is a general awareness that the translation, especially of the three "presidential prayers" of each Mass (collect i.e.,opening prayer, prayer over the offerings, prayer after communion) in many cases is too free and is near paraphrase, as well as omitting some words and phrases in the Latin original.

> When the first edition of the *Sacramentary* [i.e., the missal in English] was prepared in the early 1970s there was not time for ICEL to do scholarly background work on the *Sacramentary* texts. The new ritual books, including the *Sacramentary*, came rapidly from Rome one after the other, especially from 1969 to 1975. It was not possible for the bishops of ICEL's Board to have long, defined periods for study, comment and vote. There was an eagerness in all the conferences of bishops to have the English texts as soon as possible.

(ICEL Report to the United States Bishops' Conference, 17 June 1993, p. 3)

Revising the Missal

Over the years, there was growing awareness that a new and improved translation of the Roman Missal in English was needed.

> An essential element for the translating work of ICEL is fidelity to the substance of the original. The translation is designed to convey the content that the Latin texts embody, which in the texts of the *Proprium de tempore* [the parts of the missal that vary from day to day] includes a definite tradition of teaching and worship. The purpose of a basic textual criticism is not to ensure a literal translation (a literal translation requires little more than a few years of school Latin). Rather, this function is needed to achieve the richness and variety that is required to convey in English the true thought of the Latin text; or to make explicit, in a way that English may demand, what is cryptic or allusive in the Latin; or to permit a precise reflection of the liturgical occasion, function or context of a text; or to retain the text's theme, point of view or strength. A basic textual criticism may also be a safeguard against taking Latin words for cognates when they really are not, or against simply presuming the meaning of what looks like a familiar term.'

(Progress Report on the Revision of the Roman Missal, ICEL 1988, p.12)

So the complicated and laborious task in ICEL of preparing a revised translation of the Roman Missal began in 1982 and continued carefully until ICEL had completed its work in 1993.

Here is a description of ICEL's procedure for the revised translation of the *Missale Romanum*. The description comes from the international commission's own *Progress Report on the Revision of the Roman Missal*, 1988, pp.10-11.

In October 1982 the International Commission on English in the Liturgy issued a consultation book on the revision of the presidential prayers of the Roman Missal. The consultation book was meant to elicit comment on the revision of the 1,324 presidential prayers in the Roman Missal. Bishops, consultants and other interested persons in all of the twenty-six conferences of bishops that ICEL serves were invited to submit comments, critical or laudatory, on the Missal oration-texts issued by ICEL in 1973. The consultation period lasted over a year. One hundred and forty responses were received. Perhaps half of the respondents limited their remarks to comments on a few words or phrases in a small number of prayers. Other respondents offered extensive remarks on the 1973 Missal texts and suggested in addition some general principles for translating the collects, exemplified in a few instances by the respondents' own versions. Through most of 1984 the responses were tabulated and studied, at first within the ICEL Secretariat and then by members of ICEL's subcommittee on translations and revisions.

The first meeting of this subcommittee to discuss the approach to be taken to the revision of the Missal prayers was held in 1984. To assist its discussions the subcommittee had before it a set of guidelines for the revision of texts that had been formulated by ICEL's Advisory Committee in November 1982. By the time that the discussion on the Missal prayers took place the subcommittee had the example of the recently revised prayers of the funeral rite, the first ritual book to undergo the comprehensive process of revision announced by ICEL in 1977. The texts of the revised funeral rite embodied the decisions of the subcommittee that were to influence the approach to the prayers of the Missal: careful attention to a substantive fidelity to the Latin originals; a fuller vocabulary with a greater use of adjectives and strong verbs; greater attention to speech stresses or the rhythm and cadence of the prayers; use of connectives that results in somewhat longer sentences but conveys the subordination of ideas in the text. Yet the subcommittee also kept before it the need to measure all such decisions by the principles of the 1969 Instruction on Translation of Liturgical Texts [*Comme le prévoit*, issued by Consilium for the Implementation of the Constitution on the Sacred Liturgy] with its emphasis on the requirements of proclamation – ease for those who proclaim the texts and for those who hear them.

In general the subcommittee agreed that the approach taken in revising the funeral-rite prayers should be followed for the prayers of the Missal, but that the traditional, succinct collect-form makes greater demands on the translator than the often longer, more expanded texts of the funeral rite. The plan for revising the 1,324 prayer texts of the Missal involves the following procedures:

1 research on the background of each of the Latin texts is prepared by an expert in the ICEL Secretariat;

2 the research material is sent to 'teams' (in practice, one or two people) of translators, along with a page containing the Latin, the present ICEL text, the Italian, French and German official translations of the Missal prayers;

3 the translators prepare a draft;

4 the drafts submitted by each team of translators are reviewed by an editorial committee of three members of the subcommittee;

5 the text agreed on by the editorial committee is then

submitted for review by the full subcommittee on translations and revisions;

6 each text approved by the full subcommittee is submitted to the Advisory Committee on a page containing the Latin, present ICEL version, and the several draft versions; the text is reviewed and voted on by the Advisory Committee; texts not accepted at this stage are returned to the subcommittee until they meet with the Advisory Committee's approval;

7 texts approved by the Advisory Committee are given final review and vote by ICEL's Episcopal Board.

Throughout the long years of revision, ICEL kept its member-conferences of bishops (and the associate member-conferences) as well as the congregation in Rome informed of its work. A Progress Report on the Revision of the Roman Missal (quoted at length above) was sent to the conferences and to the Congregation for Divine Worship in 1988. Two more extensive Progress Reports were issued by ICEL in 1990 and 1992, with copies sent to the bishops and to the congregation. Through the bishops who represented their conferences on the Episcopal Board of ICEL, the conferences were apprised of the reasons for the options chosen where there could have been a variety of translations for a word, a phrase or a sentence. Beginning in 1992, the conferences were asked to give their definitive canonical vote on each completed segment (there were eight of these) as it was sent to them by the commission.

Approval of the 1998 version

Every one of the conferences voted to approve the ICEL revision. Ten of the conferences had unanimous or near-unanimous votes. The only exception was the United States, where there were a number of negative votes on one part of the ICEL text. The part in question was the very important Order of Mass, Ordo Missae, comprising the unchanging texts in Mass, including the eucharistic prayers. Even so and despite the negative votes, there was still a sufficient number of affirmative votes to secure the two-thirds majority required for approval.

After its formal approval by a conference, the final stage before the revised Roman Missal could be published for use in dioceses and churches was to apply to the Congregation for Divine Worship and the Discipline of the Sacraments for that body's confirmation (*recognitio*) of the conference's approval. The English-speaking conferences of bishops therefore submitted their requests to Rome, in 1998 or 1999 depending on each conference's voting schedule.

Five
A Cold Wind from Rome

Congregation for Divine Worship and the Discipline of the Sacraments

IT WAS THAT FINAL STAGE IN THE LONG PROCESS that caused all the bother. After the many years of work from 1982, work that involved not only the international commission but also the English-speaking conferences of bishops, the Congregation for Divine Worship and the Discipline of the Sacraments refused to give the revised translation its confirmation.

Why did this sad situation occur?

Since the Second Vatican Council (1962-1965), bishops' conferences had been submitting translated texts to the Holy See for its confirmation. Texts in English, French, German and Spanish were particularly important because they were going to be used, in each case, by a number of countries. English texts, however, that is, those which were ICEL translations, had a special importance. This was because many bishops' conferences, mainly in the developing countries of Africa and Asia, were understood to use the English texts as the basis of their translations into many local, non-European, languages.

Relations, friendly and otherwise

During the years since the Council, the Congregation for Divine Worship had generally maintained friendly and constructive relations with ICEL. There were some exceptions to this, and the reason for variations in the quality of relations, easy or difficult, seemed to depend on the cardinal who happened to be the prefect (i.e., head) of the congregation at any given time. The different attitudes of the

English-speakers who were officials in the congregation and who changed from time to time could also be very influential. Relations had been difficult in the 1980s, during the years when Cardinal James R. Knox, an Australian, was prefect. After him, and under subsequent prefects, cordial relations were resumed – until 1996. It was then that Cardinal Jorge Arturo Medina Estévez, who had been archbishop of Valparaíso in Chile, was called to the Roman Curia by Pope John Paul II and put in charge of the Congregation for Divine Worship.

It soon became clear that things were going to change. Until then, it was common for ICEL to send a few officials to Rome from time to time for informal discussions with officials of the congregation. They would speak about ICEL's work at the time and of the progress of the work; they answered questions from the congregation's representatives, heard their comments and, in a word, worked collaboratively for the good of English-speaking Catholics throughout the world.

From the start of his reign Cardinal Medina let it be known that relations with ICEL, if any, would be formal and cold. There were no further collaborative meetings, no advice or comments were forthcoming in the course of our work and, in general, we felt that we were under suspicion.

ICEL's two principal officials are, first, the chairman of its Episcopal Board and, second, the executive secretary (nowadays called 'executive director'). Since 1980 the executive secretary had been Dr John R. Page, an American layman, a wise, learned, hard-working and totally conscientious servant of the Church. The chairman of the Episcopal Board was elected for a term of two years, renewable, by his colleagues on the board. Over the years there had been some illustrious figures holding the position: Cardinal Gordon Joseph Gray, archbishop of St Andrews and Edinburgh; Archbishop Denis E. Hurley of Durban; Archbishop Daniel E. Pilarczyk of Cincinnati. The last-named left office in 1997 and I was elected to succeed him – a great honour and, as it turned out, something of a poisoned chalice (perhaps an appropriate metaphor for a liturgy appointment).

My term as chairman of ICEL saw the finishing touches put to our definitive new translation of the revised Roman Missal and its despatch to the conferences so that, as long as each had taken its formal canonical vote and the necessary majority had been obtained, the conference could then seek Rome's confirmation. In addition, we continued with work on a number of other liturgical books – some revised translations, some translations of new books issued by Rome. But during all my time in office, we were aware of the increasing hostility of the Congregation for Divine Worship. There were various demands for changes to which we attempted to respond appropriately; but the threatening situation induced in us a growing fear for the very existence of the international commission.

For example, we had done a translation of the revised Latin edition of The Rites of Ordination of a Bishop, of Priests and of Deacons. When our translation, approved by English-speaking conferences of bishops, was sent to Rome for confirmation, the response (20 September 1997) came back in very scathing terms. The translation was deemed full of unacceptable elements: errors, liberties taken with the original Latin text, unlawful changes etc. Not only was the congregation's confirmation denied, but the peremptory and unfriendly tone of the response was unprecedented and ominous.

There was an important player in the developing situation whom I have not yet mentioned. When my predecessor as ICEL chairman (Archbishop Pilarczyk) left office, he also retired from ICEL. He was succeeded, as the United States member of the Episcopal Board, by Cardinal Francis E. George O.M.I., the newly appointed archbishop of Chicago. Although he became a member of the Episcopal Board in 1997, the first meeting which he was able to attend was in summer of 1998, a few months after he had been made a cardinal.

Cardinal George arrived at that meeting straight from Rome. His message to the other bishops, members of the board, was stark and dramatic: if ICEL did not change radically, it was finished. Rome, he said, was very dissatisfied with us and its patience was not inexhaustible; moreover, the United States bishops felt that the revised missal had already been too long in its preparation. They wanted texts and, if ICEL could not oblige, they might leave the commission and provide their own translations.

Cardinal George's statement to the Episcopal Board produced very mixed, but strong, reactions – dismay, fear, anger. Apart from the dissatisfaction of Rome, the threat of United States withdrawal from ICEL was rightly seen, if it were to happen, as the end of the international commission. The United States' importance and influence in the commission (because of the size of the Church there) were far greater than those of any other bishops' conference. The rest of us could not possibly operate as an international commission without the United States, especially if the latter were operating as an alternative commission.

The Episcopal Board took a very serious view of the situation. We felt vulnerable, maligned and unjustly treated but, in the dire circumstances, we knew that we would have to do something. However, to know what we had to do was not easy to decide. Just how radical were the demands being made of us came in a letter to me from Cardinal Medina and dated 26 October 1999.

The letter of 26 October 1999

I had written to the cardinal earlier in the year, seeking (in our quandary) a meeting between some officials of the Congregation for Divine Worship and a few ICEL members. Previous meetings of this kind, when other cardinals had been in charge of the congregation, had proved very useful in a number of ways.

Cardinal Medina replied (26 October 1999), informing me that while, as a bishop, I would always be most welcome if I happened to be in Rome, the "certain steps" which his letter required to be taken by ICEL would render the larger meeting that I had proposed unnecessary at that time; and, in fact, he added, such meetings between the congregation and the commission had no formal basis and were of doubtful feasibility. His message, couched in diplomatically courteous language, clearly rebuffed my request.

The cardinal's letter went on to speak of 'the gravity of the present situation of the Mixed Commission' (the congregation seemed reluctant to use the words 'International Commission on English in the Liturgy' or even 'ICEL') and adduced a number of examples to illustrate his assertion.

ICEL's executive secretary, Dr John R. Page, was criticised for having taken 'certain liberties' (unspecified) and the Advisory Committee of ICEL lacked 'satisfactory membership'. The latter criticism implied that the committee, as well as having assumed an autonomy to which it had no right, was drawn from those who followed a liberal and progressive view of liturgical renewal and was not properly representative of other strands of thought in the Church.

The letter then accused the commission of having an attitude of arrogant intransigence. The congregation had had its communications to ICEL discussed, criticised, 'countered with unfounded charges of personal grudges and hostility to the Commission'. Moreover, 'not a few Bishops have expressed concerns, notably about the quality of the translations produced by the Mixed Commission, but also about procedures which they felt limited their own ability to obtain corrections and improvements that they considered necessary for the accuracy of the texts'.

Further examples were given in the letter to illustrate the congregation's conclusion that 'the Mixed Commission in its present form is not in a position to render…an adequate level of service'.

Claiming that 'the constitution, the regulation and the oversight of an international commission for liturgical translation are rightfully the competence of the Holy See to a degree which is not always sufficiently reflected in the Statutes which govern such bodies', Cardinal Medina declared that 'a thoroughgoing reform and revitalization of the Mixed Commission is needed'.

"For these reasons, this Congregation…hereby directs the Statutes of the 'International Commission for (sic) English in the Liturgy' be renewed thoroughly and without delay'. We were told to carry out this revision within six months 'in active consultation with this Dicastery [Congregation] and incorporating within the Constitution of the renewed Commission the considerations attached to this letter'.

These 'considerations', seven in number, were peremptory and draconian. They included the following instructions:

- ICEL was forbidden to provide any more original texts and was ordered to cease having contacts 'with bodies pertaining to non-Catholic ecclesial communities';
- 'Careful reconfiguration' of the office of executive secretary was to take place;
- ICEL employees were to be on fixed term contracts, with any extensions being reserved to the Congregation for Divine Worship;
- Everyone working for ICEL (except Episcopal Board members) had to receive clearance from the congregation;
- The redrafting of ICEL's statutes was to be done directly and exclusively by the bishops of ICEL.

One of Cardinal Medina's principal demands, as we have seen, was that ICEL's constitution be radically altered. This constitution had been formulated in ICEL's early years as a codification of what seemed necessary and right for the successful fulfilment of the tasks which the conferences of bishops had given to the commission. The constitution had worked well, it had been accepted by the conferences which ICEL served and, until the arrival of Cardinal Medina as Prefect of the Congregation for Divine Worship and the Discipline of the Sacraments, had never been criticised by Rome.

Nonetheless, we had to do something or, quite probably, perish.

The Episcopal Board held an emergency meeting in London in January 2000. It was a dismal affair in cold, dismal weather. Cardinal George introduced a document which he had prepared as a draft of a new constitution. There was reluctant acquiescence that it provided a start to our deliberations. Following the London meeting, a small group of Episcopal Board members continued the work, in contact with each other by e-mail, fax and telephone. The full Episcopal Board met again in July 2000 in California and there we pursued our difficult and, at times, unpleasant task. We managed to come to an agreement on a revised version of ICEL's constitution. This was sent to our member conferences and, most crucial of all, to the congregation in Rome, hoping that Cardinal Medina and his officials would be satisfied with our efforts.

Although the Episcopal Board complied with the congregation's demand for a thorough revision of ICEL's 'Statutes' (the congregation had told us to stop using the word 'Constitution'), we felt aggrieved and that we were being treated harshly, even unjustly. The severity of the criticisms of John Page, our executive secretary, caused great hurt, especially since the accusation that he had taken 'certain liberties' was unsubstantiated and, by us who worked with him, seen as false. The allegation that the congregation had been informed that 'not a few Bishops' were dissatisfied with ICEL and its work was strange. If 'not a few Bishops' were dissatisfied, this should have been said at meetings of their conferences and brought to our notice. But the conferences always gave ICEL their approval of its work and its productions. ICEL could not be expected to satisfy every bishop in every bishops' conference – that would have been an impossibility.

Our work in providing some 'original texts' (i.e., prayers not translated from the Latin but composed especially for the missal in English) had been included in ICEL's remit at its inception, as we have seen, and such texts were in the 1974 translation of the missal. Similar original prayers, usually alternative Opening Prayers for Sundays and feasts or some extra votive Masses, are to be found in missals in other languages also, and with the congregation's *recognitio*.

Moreover, our contacts with non-Catholic liturgical agencies had resulted in a number of agreed common texts for prayers etc. used by other Christians as well as Catholics; this ecumenical initiative was appreciated by non-Catholics and its prohibition by the Congregation for Divine Worship (contrary to the founding conferences' instructions) was a great disappointment to many non-Catholics and, in fact, also to the Holy See's Pontifical Council for the Promotion of Christian Unity.

ICEL was certainly not above criticism or incapable of improvement. We would have welcomed a broader representation of liturgy scholars as members of the very important Advisory Committee of the commission. Inevitably also, the scholarship, expertise and experience which ICEL could command (and the work committed to the commission by the conferences) might easily give the impression that the commission was making the decisions or dictating to the bishops' conferences. The latter relied on ICEL to do the work and, on the whole, appreciated what they received from the commission. We saw ourselves as serving the conferences and English-speaking Catholics the world over and we felt very privileged to have been given that task.

ICEL sought and welcomed constructive criticism of its work, but the tone of Cardinal Medina's letters and the general attitude of hostility in the Congregation for Divine Worship from 1997 onwards made things very difficult. The commission sent the congregation copies of all the *Progress Reports* and of the missal segments as they were ready; yet, during all those years of work and expense, the congregation never once moved to warn us of their views about our translation which, in the end, they found so defective. The congregation, in fact, showed little, if any, appreciation of the work done. There was no affirmation of the skill, expertise and learning of ICEL members; just peremptory and threatening demands – do this, or else…

Role of the Bishops' Conferences

One aspect of the dispute that should not be overlooked was the role of the bishops' conferences that ICEL serves.

Since the international commission had been established by the English-speaking conferences and not by the Holy See, we had understood that our 'superiors' were the conferences, which therefore had power to change the rules by which we operated as well as the personnel who worked for the commission.

Quite suddenly, the congregation declared that it was the authority to which ICEL was subject. Did this declaration not need to be discussed by the conferences and between the congregation and the conferences? Did the conferences not wonder whether there was a kind of usurpation of authority taking place, a centralisation that was removing authority rightly held by bishops' conferences in accordance with the ecclesiology of Vatican II and the principle of subsidiarity? I shall return to this matter at the end of this section.

On a number of occasions ICEL arranged for the presidents of English-speaking bishops' conferences to have worldwide telephone link-ups to discuss the crisis all together. These involved the participants having to 'meet' at different, and often very inconvenient, hours of the day or the night. Even this, we felt, was not enough, especially in the new and serious circumstances that had arisen.

Consequently, responding to a plea from me for directions from the sponsoring conferences of ICEL, the U.S. conference convened a meeting of the presidents of the conferences in Washington in Easter week, April 2000, to discuss ICEL's situation. Subsequently and again at ICEL's request, the conference presidents went twice to Rome for meetings with the Congregation for Divine Worship and also with the Congregation for Bishops. Although prior to the meetings the presidents expressed their support for the international commission and their determination 'to do something', the meetings with the congregations produced no effective results. Surely there had occurred an unwarranted extension of the aphorism, '*Roma locuta est, causa finita est*'. By the way, the congregations stipulated that no one from ICEL should take part in, or even be present at, the meetings with the presidents of the conferences!

Towards a crisis point

Cardinal Medina's letter of 26 October 1999 was the start of an intense correspondence between the congregation and ICEL. The congregation's letters were signed by the cardinal prefect or by his deputy, Archbishop Francesco Pio Tamburrino. They were addressed to me, as chairman of the Episcopal Board of ICEL. It was I who had to write on behalf of ICEL, although I consulted before doing so.

Only a month after the long letter of October 1999, there was another from the congregation directing me to send details of the steps that ICEL had taken to implement the demands of the earlier letter. I was also told to send to the congregation copies of the letters which I had written to the bishops' conferences on the subject.

Then in early December 1999 there was another letter from Cardinal Medina, telling me that my reply to his letter of 26 October was unsatisfactory. He said that there was to be no argument about the congregation's allegations concerning ICEL, that only bishops were to be involved in drawing up the new ICEL statutes, and that these latter must be ready by 26 April 2000 (i.e., six months after his October letter). His December letter went on to complain that ICEL had not yet sent to the congregation any clear idea of its plan for the new statutes and that, if we continued in this unsatisfactory way, the congregation would become more involved in our work.

Our correspondence continued on a regular basis and in similar icy terms. On 15 January 2000, for example, Archbishop Tamburrino wrote to me. The congregation's impatience and frustration are evident.

> As Your Excellency knows, over a very considerable period of time the Congregation has made sincere, repeated and patient efforts to suggest, to counsel, to prompt and to urge improvements in the policies, procedures and attitudes of the variegated and complex reality that has become known under the acronym ICEL. The issue has never been theory or questions of personality, but quite simply the question of the quality, pastoral suitability and doctrinal reliability of the translations produced by the Mixed Commission.
>
> The efforts of the Congregation have scarcely met with success. Appeals of a generic sort, detailed elucidations of problems, and pointers to faulty procedure have been of scant avail...
>
> Even though they have attempted to build on seemingly hopeful recent developments, the initiatives and requests

of the Holy See continue to meet with responses which appear, in all honesty, to be negative and obstructive, notwithstanding clear and detailed communications from the Congregation in recent months which have indicated in a confidential, dispassionate, courteous and respectful manner that the time for half-measures is now passed and that concrete solutions cannot further be delayed…

The Episcopal Board had a meeting in London in early January 2000, as I have already explained. I kept the congregation informed of this and of what progress we were making in revising the statutes of the commission. I had also to reply to a stream of letters from the congregation demanding action, seeking detailed information, threatening severe measures unless… In illustration of this, among the frequent letters received, Cardinal Medina, writing (or, rather, signing) on 19 March 2000, informed me that:

The Congregation has indicated a workable plan for remedying the problems which have arisen, but if it is not put into action expeditiously, other innovative means will have to be found to the same end. These might include the withdrawal of any degree of approbation, presumed or explicit, of the present Mixed Commission by the Congregation. This is a step which the Congregation for some time has been reluctant to take but the present difficulties regrettably bring such definitive actions to mind…

After the meeting of the Episcopal Board in San José, California, at the end of July 2000 at which we produced proposed new statutes, I wrote to Cardinal Medina and enclosed a copy of our proposals for his consideration. His reply notes some welcome progress by ICEL in meeting the congregation's demands, but there continued to be criticism, including a complaint about the long delay in responding to the congregation's instructions. It was as if the cardinal had little understanding that the Episcopal Board members were all bishops with diocesan duties and commitments and that we lived in Europe, Asia,

Africa, America and Australasia. By the way, my letter to him was sent on 30 July (the day on which our California meeting ended); the cardinal's reply, complaining of our lack of urgency, was dated 6 October.

In the final months of 2000 there were suggestions that the congregation was willing to allow, as an interim measure, a two-years trial of the new statutes of ICEL as formulated in California in July. This was confirmed to me in a letter from Cardinal Medina (6 December 2000), provided there was:

> a thorough and genuine renewal of the personnel to be involved in the preparation and administration of any translation projects [of the commission]…together with the exclusion from the same projects of those individuals heretofore involved in similar projects.

This last and new demand seemed to us to be so extreme and astonishing as to be almost outrageous. In ICEL we felt that it was time to engage the bishops' conferences in a much more involved way. ICEL was their commission. We existed to serve them and their people. They needed to know what was going on. So I wrote to the conference presidents on 8 January 2001 to tell them of the cardinal's latest demand and send them a copy of his letter. I listed the problems it caused:

- it was impossible to work without some continuity of translators and secretariat;
- the order was against natural justice, especially towards ICEL's employed staff;
- it showed lack of trust and respect towards the Episcopal Board and the conferences which had appointed the translators and the secretariat staff.

Questioning the Basics

As already indicated, there was also an important canonical question (which, in retrospect, I think we should have raised earlier in our exchanges with Rome). Did the congregation indeed have the right to issue instructions and demands to ICEL as it had been doing since Cardinal Medina became prefect? Let me explain.

The Congregation for Divine Worship and the Discipline of the Sacraments claimed that ICEL was subject to it in virtue of canon law (canons 113-118) and certain post-Vatican II papal decrees (especially the Apostolic Constitution *Pastor Bonus*, article 65). These have relevance for 'mixed commissions' (i.e., commissions which serve more than one bishops' conference) and which formally have been constituted with a juridical personality in law.

To oppose the congregation's claim, we contended that ICEL, though a mixed commission, had never been given a juridical personality and that it was never more than an agency (without juridical personality), set up to serve English-speaking conferences. The presidents of the bishops' conferences, at their meeting in Washington in April 2000, had confirmed this. Therefore, we contended that ICEL was created by, and was subject to, the bishops' conferences which had established it in 1963. Furthermore, there is no legal or other requirement that every mixed commission must have juridical personality. There is provision for such bodies without juridical personality in canon law (canon 459) and acknowledged in various papal documents and in the practice of bishops' conferences with no objection from the Holy See (intil the arrival on the scene of Cardinal Medina).

If this argument regarding ICEL's status had been accepted by the congregation, it would have meant that the latter's demand to vet and approve every person (except bishops) who worked for ICEL was illegal. Likewise, the order for ICEL to cease composing original prayers for liturgical use and to break off its ecumenical contacts would have been invalid. It would also have followed that ICEL's compliance with the instructions of the congregation was done not out of required obedience but only to foster good relations and close collaboration with the congregation.

There was yet another contentious matter. It concerns the right claimed by the Congregation for Divine Worship that all translations approved by bishops' conferences must be submitted to the congregation for its *recognitio*. The claim is based on article 36 of the Constitution on the Liturgy of the Second Vatican Council. However, although in article 36 there is an obligation on conferences to seek Holy See approval regarding *which texts* should be translated (art.36.3), there is no such obligation to have Holy See approval of the *translations made* (art.36.4) [see page 37, above.]. In fact, the Council bishops deliberately resisted an attempt to have such a requirement enacted.

How, then, did the present obligation arise to submit the translations themselves to the judgment of the Holy See? Answer: it arises from a *Motu Proprio, Sacram Liturgiam*, issued six weeks after the promulgation of the Constitution on the Liturgy. In paragraph 9 of the *Motu Proprio* are the following words:-

> Therefore it seems advisable to make it clear that vernacular versions [of the Breviary] must be drawn up and approved by the competent territorial ecclesiastical authority as provided in article 36.3 and 4 [of the Constitution on the Liturgy] and that, as provided in article 36.3, the acts of this authority require due approval, that is confirmation, of the Holy See. This is the course to be taken whenever any Latin liturgical text is translated into the vernacular by the authority already mentioned.

These words are a conflation (unconsciously or deliberately) of two different decisions in article 36 of the constitution with the result that the requirement of Holy See confirmation of a decision to put some texts into the vernacular is extended (allegedly on the authority of the Vatican II decree) to the translation itself!

Such considerations as these, in addition to the onslaught to which ICEL was being subjected by the Congregation for Divine Worship, were the background to my letter of 8 January 2001 addressed to the conference presidents. The cry for help brought a quick and heartening response from most of them. Six of the eleven replied with letters of support and agreeing that 'something must be done about this'. Another two presidents gave similar support, but orally. I had no replies from three.

Liturgiam Authenticam

Life in the International Commission on English in the Liturgy had been uncomfortable, to put it mildly, since Cardinal Medina was made head of the Congregation for Divine Worship and the Discipline of rhe Sacraments in 1996. His frequent letters contained instructions to us and demands unprecedented, threatening and ominous.

But in May 2001 the Congregation produced a new weapon to restrain and subjugate ICEL. The new weapon proved to be a disciplinary exocet missile.

This needs some explanation.

Translation from one language to another is not simply a word-for-word operation. There has to be a certain flexibility, otherwise the translation will be amateurish and will sound very stilted. Languages differ in their constructions and in their style. The translation has to be intelligible and must sound natural and not awkward and foreign. Translations of liturgical texts have also to read well when proclaimed as prayer. The optimum lies somewhere in the middle between strictly literal and word-for-word on the one hand and mere paraphrase on the other.

As guidance for those who had been given the task of translating Latin texts into vernacular languages, the Holy See published (25 January 1969) a booklet entitled *Instruction on Translation of Liturgical Texts*. It was issued by the Consilium for the Implementation of the Constitution on the Sacred Liturgy. This body, the purpose of which is obvious from its name, was established by the Holy See shortly after the Second Vatican Council. It had a separate existence until, in May 1969, it and its tasks were subsumed into the work of the Congregation for Divine Worship and the Discipline of the Sacraments.

The document came to be known as *Comme le prévoit* from its first three words in French. It is short – ten pages, 43 paragraphs – and is written in a direct and helpful way, with much common sense. It identifies the problematic issues in liturgical translations and gives guidance that is moderate and wise. The Instruction was a valuable, indeed an essential, instrument for ICEL and was constantly used and greatly appreciated.

Here, by way of illustration, are some extracts.

When a common language is spoken in several different countries, international commissions should be appointed by the conferences of bishops who speak the same language to make one text for all. (no. 2)

A faithful translation, therefore, cannot be judged on the basis of individual words; the total content of this specific act of communication must be kept in mind, as well as the literary form proper to the respective language. (no. 6)

The translator must always keep in mind that the 'unit of meaning' is not the individual word but the whole passage. He or she must therefore be careful that the translation is not so analytical that it exaggerates the importance of particular phrases while it obscures or weakens the meaning of the whole. Thus, in Latin, the piling up of *ratam, rationabilem, acceptabilem* may increase the sense of invocation. In other languages, a succession of adjectives may actually weaken the sense of the prayer. The same is true of *beatissima Virgo* or *beata et gloriosa* or the routine addition of *sanctus* or *beatus* to a saint's name, or the too casual use of superlatives. Understatement in English is sometimes the more effective means of emphasis. (no. 12)

The prayers (Opening Prayer, Prayer over the Gifts, Prayer after Communion, and Prayer over the People) from the ancient Roman tradition are succinct and abstract. In translation they may need to be rendered somewhat more freely while conserving the original ideas. This can be done by moderately amplifying them or, if necessary, paraphrasing expressions in order to concretise them for the celebration and the needs of today. In every case pompous and superfluous language should be avoided. (no. 34)

Texts translated from another language are clearly not sufficient for the celebration of a fully renewed liturgy. The creation of new texts will be necessary. But translation of texts transmitted through the tradition of the Church is the best school and discipline for the creation of new texts so 'that any new forms adopted should in some way grow organically from forms already in existence.' (Constitution *Sacrosanctum Concilium*, §23). (no. 43)

For some years before 2001 we had been advised that the Congregation for Divine Worship intended to publish a document to replace *Comme le prévoit* and update the issues involved. We were somewhat concerned in ICEL because we had, of course, been guided by *Comme le prévoit* in our revised translation of the Roman Missal. (We had been assured at the time by the then prefect of the Congregation that our work would be judged by the criteria of the earlier instruction which had been in force for the duration of the complex and costly project of the English-speaking conferences. Our translation had been completed before the successor of *Comme le prévoit* had yet appeared. In the event the assurance, which was only verbal and not in writing, was not honoured – and not even acknowledged).

The new document is dated 28 March 2001 and became effective on 25 April of that year. It is longer than its predecessor: 39 pages with a further nine pages of notes; and it has 133 paragraphs. It is more formal and legalistic throughout, from its title to its conclusion. It is headed:

FIFTH INSTRUCTION
"FOR THE RIGHT IMPLEMENTATION
OF THE CONSTITUTION ON THE SACRED LITURGY
OF THE SECOND VATICAN COUNCIL"
(Sacrosanctum Concilium, art. 36)

Liturgiam authenticam
ON THE USE OF VERNACULAR LANGUAGES
IN THE PUBLICATION OF
THE BOOKS OF THE ROMAN LITURGY

The conclusion is no less impressive:

> After the preparation of this Instruction by the Congregation for Divine Worship and the Discipline of the Sacraments in virtue of the mandate of the Supreme Pontiff transmitted in a letter of the Cardinal Secretary of State dated 1 February 1997 (Prot. n. 408.304), the same Supreme Pontiff, in an audience granted to the Cardinal Secretary of State on 20 March 2001, approved this Instruction and confirmed it by his own authority, ordering that it be published, and that it enter into force on the 25th day of April of the same year.

The Instruction is known as *Liturgiam authenticam*, the opening words of its Latin version. It is a very comprehensive document, dealing with many aspects of translation that *Comme le prévoit* had not considered. In ICEL, however, we could not but notice that all of the congregation's complaints against us with which we had become familiar through correspondence were fully included, as well as all of the demands and instructions that we had received from the congregation. It almost seemed as if ICEL had provoked the composition of *Liturgiam authenticam*. Less charitably, perhaps, it appeared that the author(s) of *Liturgiam authenticam* might have had ICEL in mind as they wrote the document. The congregation had had the text of the Missal revision in 1998 (along with requests from most of the conferences for the required *confirmatio*). Rome was silent for four years. But *Liturgiam authenticam* was issued in March 2001 and, exactly a year later, the denials of *recognitio* were being sent to the conferences.

Rules and regulations

In addition, there were other matters introduced into the new document, all of which gave a general impression of control, restriction and general negativity. Here are some passages from *Liturgiam authenticam.*

> While it is permissible to arrange the wording, the syntax and the style in such a way as to prepare a flowing vernacular text suitable to the rhythm of popular prayer, the original text, insofar as possible, must be translated integrally and in the most exact manner, without omissions or additions in terms of their content, and without paraphrases or glosses. Any adaptation to the characteristics or the nature of the various vernacular languages is to be sober and discreet. (no.20)

> Certain expressions that belong to the heritage of the whole or of a great part of the ancient Church, as well as others that have become part of the general human patrimony, are to be respected by a translation that is as literal as possible as, for example the words of the people's response *Et cum spiritu tuo*, or the expression *mea culpa, mea culpa, mea maxima culpa* in the Act of Penance in the Order of Mass. (no.56)

> ... a) The connection between various expressions, manifested by subordinate and relative clauses, the ordering of words, and various forms of parallelism, is to be maintained as completely as possible in a manner appropriate to the vernacular language.

> b) In the translation of terms contained in the original text, the same person, number and gender is to be maintained insofar as possible... (no. 57)

> The practice of seeking the *recognitio* from the Apostolic See for all translations of liturgical books accords the necessary assurance of the authenticity of the translation and its correspondence with the original texts. This practice both expresses and effects a bond of communion between the successor of blessed Peter and his brothers in the Episcopate. Furthermore, this *recognitio* is not a mere formality,

but is rather an exercise of the power of governance, which is absolutely necessary (in the absence of which the act of the Conference of Bishops entirely in no way attains legal force)… (no. 80)

The Congregation for Divine Worship and the Discipline of the Sacraments erects such 'mixed' commissions at the request of the Conferences of Bishops involved; afterwards the commission is governed by statutes approved by the Apostolic See… (no. 93)

… The Members of the Commission are always Bishops… (no. 94)

Such a Commission, in fact, insofar as possible, should exercise its office by means of the resources of the liturgical commissions of the individual Conferences involved, using their experts, their technical resources, and their secretarial staff. For example, the work undertaken is coordinated in such a way that a first draft of the translation is prepared by the liturgical commission of one Conference and then improved by the other Conferences, even in light of the diversity of expression prevailing in the same language in the individual territories. (no. 96)

In addition, the 'mixed' commissions are to limit themselves to the translation of the *editiones typicae*, leaving aside all theoretical questions not directly related to this work, and not involving themselves either in relations with other 'mixed' commissions or in the composition of original texts. (no. 98)

… These [diocesan and national] commissions shall work in their own right for the purposes proper to them, and shall not cede the matters entrusted to them to any 'mixed' commission. (no. 99)

All of the principal collaborators of any 'mixed' commission who are not Bishops, and to whom a stable mission is entrusted by such commissions, require the *nihil obstat* granted by the Congregation for Divine Worship and the Duscipline of the Sacraments before beginning their work... (no. 100)

It is to be borne in mind that the composition of new texts of prayers or rubrics is not an end in itself, but must be undertaken for the purpose of meeting a particular cultural or pastoral need. For this reason it is strictly the task of the local and national Commissions... (no. 107)

Critical reactions

On publication, the Instruction *Liturgiam authenticam* received a great deal of adverse criticism in reviews, letters to periodicals etc. Some of the criticism was directed at such matters as inconsistencies and errors in the document, excessive centralisation and micromanaging, an ethos of negativity, control and suspicion. The document appeared to deal exhaustively with practically every conceivable aspect of liturgical translation. The impression inevitably given was of a lack of respect and/or trust towards bishops' conferences and linguistic mixed commissions. Bishops and bishops' conferences seemed reduced to being the local agents of the Congregation for Divine Worship.

There was another element in *Liturgiam authenticam* that struck me as unhelpful. In many of its paragraphs, the text of the particular instruction or prohibition includes a phrase such as "in so far as this is possible" (or similar words). At first sight, this seems reasonable and wise. But, in any given case, who is to decide whether it is permissible to invoke that apparently sensible and generous concession? Answer: only the Congregation for Divine Worship and the Discipline of the Sacraments. Consequently, at the end of the long process of translation and the approval of the conferences of bishops, the congregation could decide that the 'as far as possible' phrase had been unnecessarily used; and so recognitio would be denied.

In some cases the concession obviously would have to be used. *Sursum corda* could not be rendered as 'Upwards (the) hearts'. But in most cases the congregation's opinion would be totally unknown to the translators and to the bishops' conferences – and quite likely to be strict and unyielding, even arbitrary. Hence, in order to avoid rejection at the conclusion of the whole process, the tendency would be to make the translation as literal as possible – and thus have an unsatisfactory vernacular rendering of the Latin original.

Destruction and Defeat

I have described *Liturgiam authenticam* as an exocet missile against ICEL and we certainly felt bewildered – not only the Advisory Committee and the secretarial staff but also the bishops of the Episcopal Board. Indeed, I think that the various bishops' conferences, those members at least who took a special interest in, and had real pastoral concern for, the liturgical books, above all the Roman Missal, realised the seriousness of the situation.

We really felt at a loss to know what to do or how to proceed. The conference presidents went to Rome to meet officials of the Curia, especially the Prefect of the Congregation for Bishops, but that meeting was a disappointment and inconclusive. The Episcopal Board and the Advisory Committee of ICEL tried to implement the new draft statutes. These included a provision that all the subcommittees of the Advisory Committee would be abolished, the work previously done by them to be carried out in future on a very *ad hoc* basis. This caused dismay and anger among the members of the subcommittees and only succeeded in increasing the atmosphere of gloom and despondency prevalent throughout the international commission. Whether the exocet had holed ICEL below the waterline or rendered us rudderless, we certainly felt disillusioned, hurt and abandoned.

Events then began to take over. A number of bishops who were on the Episcopal Board finished their terms of office. They were replaced by bishops who had no experience of the trials and tribulations of ICEL. Similarly with the Advisory Board where, moreover, morale was very low following the disbanding of its subcommittees and the criticism directed at it by the Congregation for Divine Worship. Efforts to recruit liturgical scholars to fill vacant places on the Advisory Board were unsuccessful – invitations were politely declined.

Another very serious development was the decision of our experienced and highly competent executive secretary, Dr John R. Page, to leave. He had been hurt and insulted by the unfair criticism of the Congregation for Divine Worship and his going was the sad loss of a much respected servant of the Church. Finally, I was 75, the age at which bishops are due to retire from diocesan responsibilities. I was of the opinion that it would not be right for ICEL to be led by a retired bishop; in addition, I had been diagnosed as suffering from cancer. When the Episcopal Board met in Ottawa in July 2002, I was receiving treatment for my illness and therefore absent from the meeting. However, in the circumstances of my age and my health, I intimated ny wish to resign as chairman and to leave the commission.

At Ottawa a new chairman of the Episcopal Board, Bishop Arthur Roche of Leeds, was elected and a new executive secretary (now called executive director) was appointed - Fr (now Mgr) Bruce Harbert, an English priest. With these new leaders and with a number of newcomers to the Episcopal Board, ICEL was able to resume operations. The changes produced a much more positive attitude on the part of the congregation in Rome and greatly improved relations between the two bodies.

As already noted, the English translation of the Roman Missal, on which ICEL had laboured since 1982 and which had been approved by all the eleven English-speaking conferences of bishops that are full members of the international commission, had been refused *recognitio* by the Congregation for Divine Worship and the Discipline of the Sacraments.

By this stage, the congregation seems to have understood and used its recognitio not merely as a kind of *nihil obstat* (i.e., that the text was free from doctrinal errors and from unacceptable omissions from, and additions to, the Latin original). *Recognitio* had apparently come to be regarded by the congregation as the right simply to dislike the translation which the conferences had approved and so, on its own authority, to consign the whole immense effort to the waste paper basket. In other words, *recognitio* had now become identified with approval. And thus the role of a bishops' conference to approve a liturgical text by its canonical vote had been abrogated.

Nonetheless, some questions remain unanswered because the congregation will not discuss them or comment. For example, when the congregation refused its *recognitio*, who exactly made that decision? Not the prefect or his deputy, because they did not speak English. A native English-speaker employed at the congregation? Whom did he consult? We are not told… The Church may not be a democracy, but surely there ought to be some willingness to be less secretive in matters such as this.

Admittedly, ICEL's stock was not high in Rome. An ICEL translation of the psalter had its *imprimatur* withdrawn by order of the Holy See. Authorities in the Roman Curia had noted that the translation of the Order of Mass had barely received the required two-thirds majority in the United States conference. And the congregation had angrily rejected an English translation of the Rites of Ordination submitted to it in the late 1990s. So one may ask, though aware that the answer will never be revealed: if the congregation had not considered itself provoked by these incidents, would it perhaps have been prepared to discuss with the conferences and seek changes in the translation of the Missal, rather than issue the draconian rejection of the whole thing in its entirety?

Finally, it is tantalising to wonder how the congregation, or indeed the Holy See itself, would have reacted if the conferences of bishops, or even the conference presidents, had claimed that their legitimate authority had been infringed by the congregation's behaviour. Such a complaint was not, I think, put forward strongly enough. If it had been, is it too fanciful to dream that it might have led to a thorough examination of the role and activities of the Roman Curia?

THE 'BANNED' TRANSLATION OF 1998

Although sadly of only academic interest, it can be interesting to examine the 'banned' translation, especially in comparison with the 1972 version and the Latin texts. Here are a few examples. (The new, acceptable translation could not be reproduced here as it had not been fully approved at time of printing.)

4th Sunday, Ordinary Time (Opening Prayer)

Latin Text

Concede nobis, Domine Deus noster,
ut te tota mente veneremur
et omnes homines rationabili diligamus affectu.

1972 Translation

Lord our God,
help us to love you with all our hearts
and to love all men as you love them.

1998 Translation

Teach us, Lord God,
to worship you with undivided hearts
and to cherish all people with true and faithful love.

17th Sunday, Ordinary Time (Opening Prayer)

Latin Text

Protector in te sperantium, Deus,
sine quo nihil est validum, nihil sanctum,
multiplica super nos misericordiam tuam
ut, te rectore, te duce,
sic bonis transeuntibus nunc utamur,
ut iam possimus inhaerere mansuris.

1972 Translation

God our Father and protector,
without you nothing is holy, nothing has value,

guide us to everlasting life
by helping us to use wisely
the blessings you have given to the world.

1998 Translation

O God,
protector of those who hope in you,
without whom nothing is strong, nothing is holy,
enfold us in your gracious care and mercy,
that with you as our ruler and guide,
we may use wisely the gifts of this passing world
and fix our hearts even now on those which last for ever.

32nd Sunday, Ordinary Time (Prayer after Communion)

Latin Text

Gratias tibi, Domine, referimus
sacro munere vegetati,
tuam clementiam implorantes,
ut, per infusionem Spiritus tui,
in quibus caelestis virtus introivit,
sinceritatis gratia perseveret.

1972 Translation

Lord,
we thank you for the nourishment you give us
through your holy gift.
Pour out your Spirit upon us
and in the strength of this food from heaven
keep us single-minded in your service.

1998 Translation

Strengthened by this holy food, O Lord,
we give you thanks and seek your mercy,
that, through the outpouring of your Spirit,
those who have been touched by the power of this sacrament
may continue to live in sincerity and truth.

The 1998 (rejected) Missal also had a number of Original Texts (i.e., texts not in the Latin Missal but newly composed by ICEL and approved by the English-speaking bishops' conferences). They were mainly Opening Prayers with a special relevance to the Readings of the Sunday or Feast which were to follow. Here are a couple of examples.

For the Second Sunday of Advent (Year C) when the gospel is John the Baptist's preaching (Luke 3:1-6):

God of our salvation,
you straighten the winding ways of our hearts
and smooth the paths made rough by sin.
Make our conduct blameless,
keep our hearts watchful in holiness,
and bring to perfection the good you have begun in us.
We ask this through him whose coming is certain, whose day
draws near;
your Son, our Lord Jesus Christ,
who lives and reigns with you in the unity of the Holy Spirit,
God for ever and ever.

For the Third Sunday of Easter (Year A) when the gospel is the Emmaus story (Luke 24:13-35):

O God of mystery,
out of death you delivered Christ Jesus,
and he walked in hidden glory among his disciples.
Stir up our faith,
that our hearts may burn within us
at the sound of his word,
and our eyes be opened to recognise him
in the breaking of the bread.
Grant this through Jesus Christ, firstborn from the dead,
who lives with you now and always in the unity of the Holy Spirit,
God for ever and ever.

In addition, the 1998 Missal contained original Collects for the following contemporary needs which may occur from time to time (and are not found in the Latin text of the Missal).

For a reverent use of creation

For victims of abuse

For the homeless

For victims of addiction

In times of epidemic

Six

John Paul II and Benedict XVI on the Mass

Two recent Papal documents

GIVEN THE IMPORTANCE, THE PROMINENCE AND THE CENTRALITY of the Eucharist in the life of Catholics and in the teaching of the Church, it is evident that there will be a great many official documents and statements on the subject. In recent years in particular we have been given an abundance of formal teaching on the Eucharist, especially from Pope John Paul II and Pope Benedict XVI.

For our purposes here, it is beyond our needs to attempt to take notice of all, or nearly all, of these recent official teachings. However, I do want to study two of the documents. One is the Apostolic Exhortation *Sacramentum Caritatis* of Benedict XVI, written after the Synod of Bishops, held in 2005 on the subject of the Eucharist. The other is the shorter Apostolic Letter of John Paul II, entitled *Mane Nobiscum Domine* and published in October 2004 to inaugurate the Year of the Eucharist (October 2004 to October 2005).

My aim is to note the points in these two documents that, for the ordinary active and concerned Catholic, the 'person in the pew', may have particular interest or relevance. Let us take the earlier and shorter document first and discover, or remind ourselves, of its teaching.

Apostolic Letter *Mane Nobiscum Domine*

Despite the specific occasion for which this Letter was written, it has timeless relevance for our appreciation and love of the Eucharist. Its title (*Mane Nobiscum Domine* = Stay With Us, Lord) indicates that Pope John Paul II proposes the Emmaus story (Lk 24:13-35) as the guide for our understanding and living out of the Eucharist. 'Stay with us, Lord, for it is almost evening'. Jesus agreed to this request and he remained with the disciples; soon, however, his presence, no longer visible but hidden, continued in 'the breaking of the bread', the very action which opened their eyes and their minds to recognise who he was. (§1)

'The Divine Wayfarer', as the Apostolic Letter calls Jesus, still walks with us, explaining the Scriptures and leading us to a deeper appreciation of the mysteries of God's love for us.

Pope John Paul briefly reviews the Church's tradition and teaching on the Eucharist. In the early centuries it was frequently called 'the Breaking of Bread' and it has always been at the centre of the Church's life and worship. In the Eucharist, Jesus makes present the 'mystery' (i.e., the fact and also the meaning) of his death and resurrection; he is received as the living bread, the bread of life, and is given to us for our spiritual nourishment and growth and as a pledge and foretaste of eternal life.

Following an Introduction, there are four sections to the Apostolic Letter. In the first, entitled 'In the Wake of the Council and the Great Jubilee', the Pope provides a short review of eucharistic events from the time of the Second Vatican Council (1962-1965). He highlights the Council itself, the encyclical letter *Redemptor Hominis*, the Jubilee Year 2000 with the Apostolic Letters *Tertio Millennio Adveniente* and *Novo Millennio Ineunte*, the International Eucharistic Congress in Rome, and the encyclical letter *Ecclesia de Eucharistia* (§§6-10). Then come the three sections which have timeless relevance.

The Eucharist, a mystery of light

What is meant by stating that the Eucharist is a mystery of light? Pope John Paul's response seems almost contradictory:

> ...in the Eucharist the glory of Christ remains veiled. The Eucharist is pre-eminently a *mysterium fidei*. Through the mystery of his complete hiddenness, Christ becomes a mystery of light, thanks to which believers are led into the depths of the divine life. (§11)

However, he clarifies these enigmatic words. On the road to Emmaus, Jesus explains to the distraught disciples how all the Scriptures point to the mystery of his own person. In a similar manner, in the sixth chapter of St John's gospel, Jesus speaks of the mystery of his person (who he is) before revealing the presence of himself as the eucharistic food of life. In the Mass we have the same sequence. The 'table of the word' always precedes the 'table of the Eucharist'. What we hear in the former throws light on the latter. The Eucharist, the 'mystery of faith', becomes also a 'mystery of light'.

The Second Vatican Council emphasised the importance of the Liturgy of the Word. It introduced a wider and more orderly selection of biblical passages and ruled that they should be proclaimed in the people's own language. The Council also said that the homily was to be part of the liturgy and that it should explain the Scripture readings and show their relevance to our lives. The Pope reiterates these points and urges that the Scriptures should be proclaimed well, with great care and preparation, and that meditative silences should be observed to allow what they have heard to reach people's minds and hearts.

The two disciples at Emmaus had been prepared by the Lord's words on the way there. Hence they were able to recognise him by his simple gesture of breaking the bread. Likewise, when we have been prepared by the Liturgy of the Word at Mass,

> signs begin to 'speak'. The Eucharist unfolds in a dynamic context of signs… Through these signs the mystery in some way opens up before the eyes of the believer. (§14)

The most obvious fact about the Eucharist is that it is a meal. As such, it is an effective sign of our fellowship with God and with one another. But the Eucharist also

> has a profoundly and primarily sacrificial meaning. In the Eucharist, Christ makes present to us anew the sacrifice offered once for all on Golgotha. Present in the Eucharist as the risen Lord, he nonetheless bears the marks of his passion

of which every Mass is a 'memorial'. (§15)

Furthermore, the Eucharist has an eschatological aspect, directing our thoughts to the future when Christ will come again; thus our minds are filled with hope.

Pope John Paul speaks of all these dimensions coming together

in one aspect which more than any other makes a demand on our faith: the mystery of the 'real' presence. (§16)

The adjective 'real' does not deny Christ's real presence among us in other ways; it means that his real presence in the Eucharist is real *par excellence*. 'He becomes substantially present, whole and entire, in the reality of his body and blood' (§16). It is this real presence of Jesus that gives all three aspects of the Eucharist already described a significance beyond symbolism.

It follows, therefore, that the Eucharist, the great mystery at the centre of our lives as Christians, must always be well celebrated by everyone who participates. The General Instruction of the Roman Missal must be studied and its precepts observed. The faithful should be instructed so that they are enabled to take their full and active part in the liturgy.

We must be fully aware that Jesus is truly present in the Eucharist and that we should behave accordingly, with deep respect and reverence; it is important to allow moments of silence during the liturgy. This applies to our celebration of the Eucharist but it is also true of our eucharistic adoration outside of Mass. Such adoration has a special purpose of making reparation, by acts of faith and love, for the lack of respect frequently shown to our Lord and for the neglect and even the insults that are so widespread.

Time spent before Jesus in the Blessed Sacrament also, of course, deepens our communal and personal relationship with the Lord and nourishes our faith and our love for him. Among the various aids to eucharistic devotion, the Pope makes special mention of the Rosary, recited 'in the biblical and christocentric form...with Mary as our companion and guide'. (§18)

The Eucharist, source and manifestation of communion

The Eucharist means that Christ is not only 'with us' but, even better, 'in us'. This is the intimate union that Jesus seeks: 'Abide in me and I in you' (John 15:4). It is a union which is a foretaste of the union we shall have in heaven, the vision for which we yearn.

Since the Church is the Body of Christ, our union with Jesus in the Eucharist entails also ecclesial communion; we are in union with the Church, a unity created and intensified by the Holy Spirit. Partaking of the one eucharistic bread, the many become one body (cf. 1 Cor 10:17). It is this unity for which Christ prayed at the Last Supper (John 17:21).

Since the Eucharist is both sign and source of ecclesial unity, 'the Church sets conditions for full participation in the celebration of the Eucharist' (§21). These conditions help us to be aware of the demands of eucharistic communion: that it is hierarchical (with a range of roles and ministries) and fraternal (open, affectionate, forgiving).

In the Acts of the Apostles we are given models of ecclesial communion in the early Church (Acts 2:42-47; 4:32-35). We should try to imitate these ideals as closely as possible, especially in eucharistic celebrations of the whole diocese (cf. Constitution on the Sacred Liturgy, *Sacrosanctum Concilium*, §41). In addition, Sunday is the day of the Lord, the day of the Church. On that day the eucharistic assembly has a special significance as we recall how the apostles and disciples were gathered together on the evening of Easter Sunday and the risen Lord Jesus came into their midst.

The Eucharist, principle and plan of mission

When the two disciples had recognised Jesus as their companion at Emmaus, 'they set out immediately' to tell the other disciples that they had seen and been with the Lord. Similarly, after our celebrations, we should feel the same urge to tell others of our experience. For us all there is 'an urgent summons to testimony and evangelisation' (§24). Indeed, the dismissal at the end of Mass (*Ite, missa est*:

'Go, the Mass is ended' or, better, 'Go forth, the Mass is ended') 'is a charge to work for the spread of the gospel and the imbuing of society with Christian values'. (§24)

The Eucharist gives us not only the strength for our mission, but also its pattern. In other words, we proclaim to the world the 'way of living' learned from Jesus and to be imitated by us. Such a 'mode of being' comprises the values expressed by the Eucharist, the attitudes and resolutions it inspires.

A basic element in all this is thanksgiving (the etymological meaning of the word 'Eucharist'). In the unconditional and obedient 'yes' of Jesus to the Father's will, our 'yes' and 'thank you' and 'amen' are contained. In a world where secularism is so prevalent and God is ignored, our constant witness of giving thanks to God is a necessary assertion that 'human reality cannot be justified without reference to the Creator' (cf. Pastoral Constitution on the Church in the Modern World, *Gaudium et Spes*, §36). (§26)

Therefore, Pope John Paul continues,

> Christians ought to be committed to bearing more forceful witness to God's presence in the world. We should not be afraid to speak about God and to bear proud witness to our faith. (§26)

When celebrating the Eucharist we must be aware of the unity of the entire human race. The Eucharist should be 'a project of solidarity' towards all of humanity. We are called to be 'promoters of communion, peace and solidarity in every situation…and promoters of dialogue and communion'. (§27)

Furthermore, the Eucharist impels us to 'practical commitment to building a more just and fraternal society' (§28). The Eucharist shows us a God who loves us without limit. At its institution Jesus, the apostles' master and teacher, knelt down to wash their feet (John 13:1-20). By so doing, he explains unequivocally the meaning of the Eucharist. Can we not do something to alleviate the poverty of so many of our brothers and sisters? The tragedies of hunger, disease, loneliness, unemployment and exile are scandals in a world of so much wealth. By our concern for the victims of these evils we shall be recognised as true followers of Christ. 'This will be the criterion by which the authenticity of our eucharistic celebrations will be judged'. (§28)

Conclusion

We are called 'to grow in awareness of the incomparable treasure which Christ has entrusted to his Church' (§29). The Pope asks for a more fervent celebration of the Eucharist and an increase of eucharistic devotion outside of Mass. He invites priests ('who repeat the words of consecration each day and are witnesses and heralds of the great miracle of love which takes place at [their] hands') to celebrate their daily Masses as joyfully and devoutly as they did their first Mass and to spend time in prayer before the tabernacle. He urges readers and extraordinary ministers of the Eucharist

> to become ever more aware of the gift you have received in the service entrusted to you for a more worthy celebration of the Eucharist'.

Finally,

> may all of you, the Christian faithful, rediscover the gift of the Eucharist as light and strength for your daily lives in the world, in the exercise of your respective professions amid so many different situations'. (§30)

Invoking the Blessed Virgin Mary, 'whose whole life incarnated the meaning of the Eucharist' and who gave birth to him who is the Eucharist, Pope John Paul II concludes his Apostolic Letter with these words:

> Sustained by Mary, may the Church discover new enthusiasm for her mission and come to acknowledge ever more fully that the Eucharist is the source and summit of her entire life. (§31)

Apostolic Exhortation *Sacramentum Caritatis*

The Apostolic Exhortation *Sacramentum Caritatis* is a much longer document than *Mane Nobiscum Domine*. In it Pope Benedict's scriptural erudition and theological scholarship are immediately evident. Parts of the document are very cerebral and therefore sometimes a challenge to the reader trying to follow the train of Pope Benedict's thought.

Sacramentum Caritatis is divided into three parts, allowing the Pope to cover very comprehensively the Church's eucharistic teaching and practice. The three sections are: 1) The Eucharist: a Mystery to be Believed; 2) The Eucharist: a Mystery to be Celebrated; 3) The Eucharist: a Mystery to be Lived.

Here is an attempt to summarise, as helpfully as possible, this challenging document.

PART ONE. THE EUCHARIST: A MYSTERY TO BE BELIEVED

Pope Benedict declares:

> The Church's faith is essentially a eucharistic faith and it is especially nourished at the table of the Eucharist. (§6)

Hence this first section consists of a series of reflections in which the relationships are traced between the Eucharist, on the one hand, and the Trinity, the Church, the other sacraments, eternal life and the Blessed Virgin. Let us name and briefly illustrate the Pope's teaching on these multiple relationships inherent in the Eucharist.

• **The Eucharist is a gift of the Trinity to the Church and to God's people.**

The entire history of salvation is the result of God's loving plan. Jesus Christ incarnate, come to save us, is the greatest element in that plan. The Eucharist is the continuing presence of the risen Saviour, the Trinity's loving gift. 'God so loved the world that he gave his only Son…' (John 3:16) and 'My Father gives you the true bread from heaven…' (John 6:32). As the Pope says, 'The 'Mystery of Faith' is thus a mystery of Trinitarian love' (§8).

• The Eucharist's relation to Jesus Christ is one of identity.

In the shedding of his blood, Jesus is the true 'Lamb of God who takes away the sins of the world'. In the mystery of his death on the cross, the new covenant binding God and man for ever is brought about. At the Jewish ritual meal when Jesus and the apostles ate together, the meal we call the Last Supper, Jesus revealed himself as the true sacrificial lamb. 'In instituting the Eucharist, Jesus anticipates and makes present the sacrifice of the cross and the victory of the resurrection' (§10). When the Church celebrates the Eucharist in response to the Lord's command, we make the paschal mystery of Christ's death and resurrection present sacramentally. Indeed, in the Eucharist we are drawn into Jesus' act of self-oblation; 'we enter into the very dynamic of his self-giving' (§11).

The Holy Spirit was present throughout the life of Jesus and 'it is through the working of the Spirit that Christ himself continues to be present and active in his Church' (§12). **The Holy Spirit plays an essential role in the Eucharist,** in particular when the bread and wine are changed into the risen and living Christ. At the epiclesis the priest explicitly prays to the Father to 'send down the gift of the Spirit so that the bread and wine will become the body and blood of Jesus Christ and that the community as a whole will become ever more the body of Christ' (§13). It is important that, at Mass, we pay full attention to the epiclesis, the invocation of the Holy Spirit upon the gifts and upon ourselves.

That there is **an intimate relationship between the Eucharist and the Church** is evident. It is, in fact, a relationship of cause and effect. 'In the sacrifice of the cross Christ gave birth to the Church as his bride and as his body...' and 'the Eucharist makes present Christ's redeeming sacrifice' (§14). The Pope remarks on the 'interplay' between the Eucharist and the Church: the Eucharist builds up the Church while the Church 'makes' the Eucharist – but the primary causality belongs to the Eucharist.

There is a further consideration to be kept in mind when reflecting on the relation between Eucharist and Church. It is the former which gives unity to the faithful in the communion that is the Church. 'The oneness of the eucharistic body of the Lord implies the oneness of his mystical body,' the Church (§15).

• The Eucharist and the other sacraments

The Apostolic Exhortation then proceeds to trace the relationship that exists between the Eucharist and each of the other sacraments. Here are some of the points made.

Since the Eucharist is the culmination of our initiation into full membership of the Church, the sacraments of baptism and confirmation, as the first two stages of initiation, are ordered or pointed towards reception of the Eucharist, which is the centre and goal of all sacramental life (§17). The document makes two important pastoral points: first, we should be very aware that reception of baptism, confirmation and Eucharist are the one process, the process of Christian initiation, 'with the Eucharist as the goal of the whole process' (§18); and second, that the process of initiation, and particularly first communion, ought to involve one's whole family (which should receive support to fulfil its educational role) (§19).

There is an intrinsic relationship between the Eucharist and the sacrament of reconciliation. *Sacramentum Caritatis* speaks of the need to restore a sense of sin in today's world and reminds us that to receive holy communion we ought to be in a state of grace. Moreover, just as the Eucharist is not something merely individual, so also every sin has a wider, social dimension than the merely personal; it damages the ecclecial communion we enter through baptism.

A pastoral request follows: that the value of this sacrament of reconciliation be emphasised and its use encouraged in dioceses and parishes. The Pope urges that the sacrament be celebrated in accordance with the Church's regulations. Finally, he recommends the 'balanced and sound practice of gaining indulgences'. Indulgences, as well as showing that, as individuals, we cannot make full reparation for our wrongdoing, also illustrate the doctrines of Christ's limitless merits and of the communion of saints (§21).

The connection between the Eucharist and the sacrament of anointing of the sick is clear. The Church's care of the sick involves both sacraments; the Eucharist is given as viaticum in the case of a dying person. Further, anointing 'unites the sick with Christ's self-offering' so that they 'can participate in the redemption of the world', brought about by Christ's paschal mystery made present for us in the Eucharist (§22).

> The intrinsic relationship between the Eucharist and the sacrament of holy orders clearly emerges from Jesus' own words in the upper room: 'Do this in memory of me' (Lk 22.19)... On the night before he died, Jesus instituted the Eucharist and, at the same time, established the priesthood of the new covenant. (§23)

At the celebration of the Eucharist, the priest presides in the person of Christ and acts in his name as well as in the name of the whole Church. Consequently, the priest must never make himself the centre of the liturgical action. He must avoid any attempt to give undue emphasis to his own personality.

The document once again stresses the importance and value of the obligation and practice of priestly celibacy in the Latin tradition. Celibacy is 'a sign expressing total and exclusive devotion to Christ, to the Church and to the Kingdom of God' (§24).

Writing of the shortage of priests in many (but not all) dioceses, Pope Benedict urges that efforts be made to encourage greater awareness of the problem; he stresses the need to promote and nurture vocations in those who give signs of being called by God to the ministerial priesthood. While bishops must never ordain anyone whose suitability is not assured, dioceses and congregations which can help should be willing to share their resources of priests with areas of scarcity.

In regard to the sacrament of matrimony, the Apostolic Exhortation speaks of the Eucharist as a nuptial sacrament. In explanation of this, we read:

> The mutual consent that husband and wife exchange in Christ, which establishes them as a communion of life and

love. also has a eucharistic dimension. Indeed, in the theology of Saint Paul, conjugal love is a sign of Christ's love for his Church, a love culminating in the cross, the expression of his 'marriage' with humanity and at the same time the origin and heart of the Eucharist. (§27)

Just as the bond uniting Christ and the Church is indissoluble, exclusive and faithful, so also these same qualities are found in marriage. This teaching of the Church on marriage can lead to serious and painful situations for some people. There is no change in the Church's discipline regarding 'this complex and troubling pastoral problem'; those in irregular marriage situations should not receive holy communion but, nonetheless, they should be earnestly encouraged to see themselves as loved and respected members of the Church. Suitable care and guidance must be available for them. Similarly, 'maximum pastoral attention' should be given to those who are preparing for marriage; their awareness of the obligations needed for validity of the sacrament of matrimony should be carefully ascertained.

• Relationship of the Eucharist with eternal life and with Mary

Finally in Part One of the Apostolic Exhortation, the Holy Father speaks of the connection between the Eucharist and eschatology and of the relationship between the Eucharist and Our Lady.

The Eucharist is both food for our continuing pilgrimage through life and a foretaste of the 'eschatological fulfilment' of our earthly journey. Celebrating the Eucharist strengthens our hope of resurrection and the joyful prospect of meeting once again those 'who have gone before us, marked with the sign of faith'. It also reminds us of the importance of prayer, especially the offering of Mass, for those who have died 'so that, once purified, they can come to the beatific vision of God' (§32).

Mary, Mother of God, now assumed to heaven, is for us a sign of sure hope of the destiny that awaits us all and of which the Eucharist gives us a foretaste. In Mary, God's gifts are completely fulfilled. Totally conformed to the Father's will, intimately united to him and his Son, filled with the Holy Spirit, Mary is an icon and a model for us who are privileged to receive the gift that Jesus makes of himself in the Eucharist.

Some observations on Part One

In this part of the post-synodal Apostolic Exhortation *Sacramentum Caritatis* Pope Benedict XVI is writing of 'The Eucharist: A Mystery to be Believed'. He is therefore speaking of the faith of the Church in regard to the Eucharist.

It is noteworthy that much of the Pope's teaching is about the relationship between the Eucharist and other elements of the Church's faith. In other words, the full importance of the Eucharist will not be appreciated if we consider it in isolation. It is true that, even when we prescind from other doctrines, the Eucharist is a most wonderful gift for us to have, a worthy method of offering to God our worship and gratitude; it is a truly effective means of seeking God's help for ourselves and for others, both living and dead; and it is the firm assurance of the risen Lord's presence and activity in our midst.

But the Apostolic Exhortation extends our appreciation of what the Eucharist is – how it is intimately connected with each of the other sacraments; how it is the essential element of the Church's life; how it connects us with the paschal mystery of Christ's death and resurrection, as well as being a foretaste and pledge of the eternal life that awaits us. All of that and, even more basic, the Eucharist brings us into intimate relationship with the Trinity: Jesus Christ, the Son of God, inseparably united to the Father and the Spirit, leads us into the presence, love and care of the Blessed Trinity.

Much of the basic theology of the Eucharist, as found in full treatises on the subject or even as contained in the Catechism of the Catholic Church, is not to be found, explicitly at least, in the Apostolic Exhortation. The Pope apparently felt it unnecessary to go into detail in this way. His teaching presumes such matters to be known and accepted. The aspects of eucharistic faith which the document emphasises are less familiar, perhaps more profound – more arcane, even – but, for such very reasons, helpful, interesting and welcome. Nor is this first part of the Apostolic Exhortation devoid of practical guidance for circumstances and situations which arise from time to time.

PART TWO. THE EUCHARIST: A MYSTERY TO BE CELEBRATED

Whereas, in Part One of the Apostolic Exhortation, Pope Benedict is very much the teacher ('The Eucharist: a Mystery to be Believed'), Part Two rather sees him as our liturgical guide. There is still, of course, much reflection and teaching on a theological understanding of the Eucharist, but the emphasis is practical: the correct and worthy celebration of Mass; the opportunities we have of making such celebrations genuine worship of a loving God; and the effective fulfilment of the Church's wish that Mass should enable all present to participate actively and fruitfully.

Part Two begins with some basic statements. First, there is an intrinsic connection between the Eucharist and our faith, and our worship expresses that faith; 'our faith and the eucharistic liturgy both have their source in the same event - Christ's gift of himself in the paschal mystery' (§34). Second, since Christ is the full manifestation of the glory and the beauty of God, the celebration of the Eucharist enables us to glimpse that divine glory and beauty; consequently, if the liturgy is to show forth its innate splendour, it must be carried out with great care.

The section continues with some general principles about the celebration of the Eucharist. It is 'the whole Christ' who celebrates, head and body, because Jesus assimilates us into himself in the sacrificial offering; it is the risen Lord who is present and who celebrates the Eucharist; for this reason its basic structure cannot be changed; and it is on Sunday, the day of the Resurrection, that the Christian community assembles to celebrate the Eucharist.

The bishop in his diocese is the chief celebrant of the Eucharist. It is his responsibility to ensure that the Eucharist is celebrated carefully and properly in the diocese. When he celebrates in the cathedral church, the liturgy ought to be a model for the whole diocese.

The Exhortation stresses the importance of words and signs in liturgical celebration; both should be used with care and dignity so that they may enable those present to participate in a manner proper to them. Likewise, liturgical art and liturgical song both have effective roles to play in the celebration of the Church's liturgy.

The different parts of the Mass

These introductory paragraphs are followed by a review of the structure and different parts of the Mass, based largely on the *General Instruction of the Roman Missal*. Let us select some of the points made by Pope Benedict.

1. The Liturgy of the Word and the Eucharistic Liturgy are two parts of the one rite, one single act of worship. There is an intrinsic bond between the two, the word of God leading us naturally into the Eucharist.

2. Since, in the Liturgy of the Word, God speaks to his people, that part of Mass must be diligently prepared and celebrated, with competent readers conscious of their responsibility. The faithful should be enabled and encouraged to appreciate the riches of sacred scripture to be found in the lectionary.

3. 'The quality of homilies needs to be improved' (§46) so that a deeper understanding of the word of God can be fostered in the faithful.

4. The presentation of the gifts is a simple but very meaningful rite because the bread and wine symbolically contain all creation to be transformed by Christ, as well as all pain and suffering in the world. In this rite, human labour is given authentic meaning as being in union with Christ's redemptive work.

5. The Eucharistic Prayer has various elements which, if we appreciate them, enable us to grasp the richness of this 'centre and summit of the entire celebration': thanksgiving, acclamation, epiclesis, institution narrative and consecration, anamnesis, offering, intercessions, final doxology.

6. The sign of peace reminds us that the Eucharist is the sacrament of peace. The sign expresses our desire and our need for the gift of peace in our world. The gesture should be restrained so that exaggeration and distraction are avoided.

7. Holy Communion is a personal encounter with the Lord Jesus in the sacrament. The method of distributing holy communion

should conform with liturgical norms. Catholics who are not in a suitable spiritual condition should not receive the sacrament. Neither should those 'of other Christian confessions' (except in certain special cases) 'and even other religions'; they should be made courteously aware that our Church lays down certain conditions that are required for reception of the sacrament.

8. The dismissal should be understood as a sending forth on mission since this is an essential element in the Church's life. As Christians we have a mission in the world and the connection between this and our celebration of Mass should be appreciated.

The meaning of 'participation'

The document then goes on to explain the meaning of that authentic participation in the Eucharist that those present should have. Vatican II called for 'active, full and fruitful participation' which is not restricted to those with ministries or roles to fulfil. All who are present should be instructed and nourished so that

> offering the immaculate Victim, not only through the hands
> of the priest but also together with him, they should learn
> to make an offering of themselves. (§52)

The beauty and harmony of the liturgy require clarity regarding the different roles of those participating. The priest presides throughout the whole of the Eucharist. 'He represents Jesus Christ, the head of the Church and, in a specific way, also the Church herself' (§53).

The Eucharist should be embedded in people's lives by inculturation:

> A more effective participation of the faithful in the holy
> mysteries will benefit from a continued inculturation of the
> eucharistic celebration. (§54)

Such inculturation should be in accordance with the Church's norms and directives.

Genuine participation in the Eucharist demands a spirit seeking constant conversion, an interior disposition fostered by an appropriate preparation for taking part in the celebration, a heart reconciled to

God. Active participation also needs to be accompanied by an effort to be involved in the life of the Church as a whole, including its missionary commitment. Full participation clearly involves the reception of holy communion; however, in cases where this is not possible, a person should make an act of spiritual communion, a desire to be fully united with Christ.

The Catholic Church holds that eucharistic communion and ecclesial communion are intrinsically linked; the Eucharist which manifests our personal communion with Jesus also implies full communion with the Church. Generally, therefore, and with regret and courtesy, we do not invite non-Catholics to receive the Eucharist. The sadness which this causes should make us look forward prayerfully to the day when all Christians will be able to celebrate and receive the Eucharist together.

Pope Benedict also writes of the importance of the Eucharist in the lives of the sick and housebound, of prisoners and of migrants. He offers guidance on large scale and small group celebrations of the Eucharist and on broadcasts of the Mass on radio and television.

He reminds us of the place that Latin has in the Church's liturgy and asks that it should be used in international Masses. More generally, people should be 'taught to recite the more common prayers in Latin and also to sing parts of the liturgy to Gregorian chant' (§62).

Interior participation

After his teaching on the 'active participation' in the Eucharist which Vatican II and subsequent documents have sought, the Pope deals with the 'interior participation' which should also occur.

If our participation is to be truly fruitful, we have to be conformed to the mystery that we are celebrating, offering our lives to God in union with Christ's self-sacrifice for the world's salvation. To achieve this, catechesis is necessary. The best method for such catechesis is *mystagogical*, i.e., the Eucharist itself provides us with the instruction needed to help us to enter more deeply into the mystery being celebrated.

To be effective, such 'mystagogical catechesis' has to

(1) be able to interpret the rites in the light of the events of the salvation story;

(2) make us more sensitive to the language and meaning of signs and gestures in the liturgy; and

(3) enable us to discern the significance of the rites for all areas and aspects of our lives. The aim ts to make our faith an adult faith able to bear witness in our world to the Christian hope that inspires us.

The Pope desires that, as a result of eucharistic catechesis, there will be an increased sense of the mystery of God's presence among us and a greater reverence for the Eucharist, shown by signs and gestures.

Eucharistic devotion

As a postscript to this section on the Eucharist as a mystery to be celebrated, there are some paragraphs on eucharistic adoration and devotion.

There is a renewed awareness of the intrinsic relation between Mass and the adoration of the Blessed Sacrament. The Mass itself is an act of adoration; and 'holy communion allows us to adore him whom we receive'. Adoration outside of Mass prolongs and intensifies this. Eucharistic adoration is the natural consequence of eucharistic celebration. Therefore, adoration of the Blessed Sacrament should be promoted among priests and the faithful, both adults and children. Adoration can take place in private visits and also in more communal ways. There are, for example, various devotions such as processions, Forty Hours and eucharistic congresses, suitably updated and adapted to local circumstances.

A short paragraph on the location of the tabernacle concludes this section of the Apostolic Exhortation. The tabernacle should be readily visible to everyone entering the church. Its location will be either in a Blessed Sacrament chapel (preferably near the sanctuary) or in a prominent place in the sanctuary itself. A suitable place for the tabernacle is necessary so that the Blessed Sacrament may receive due reverence and so that there may be opportunity for adoration.

Twenty Suggestions and Reminders

To complement Pope Benedict's teaching on the various parts of Mass, I add some points which may help us in our desire to celebrate the Eucharist as correctly and devoutly as possible. These points are mainly for Sundays.

1. Everyone, and especially those who have ministries or other roles to carry out, should be properly prepared and should be present some time before Mass is due to begin. This applies to priest, readers, servers, extraordinary ministers of the Eucharist, musicians, cantors, choir, passkeepers and welcomers.

2. The entrance procession should be accompanied by suitable music, either instrumental or sung.

3. A Liturgy of the Word for children can take place sometimes, but not on every Sunday. It is meant for children of at least primary school age. Suitable material and content of sufficient maturity should be used. (Pre-school children may have a separate assembly.)

4. The penitential rite can be varied. (A rite of sprinkling with holy water can be used occasionally.) The invocations, if the Third Form is used, can be varied, as appropriate; they are a litany to Christ – not to the Trinity and not in a form such as 'For the times that we…'.

5. Parts of Mass should be sung. Top priority should be given to singing the 'ordinary', especially the acclamations (Gloria; Gospel Acclamation; Holy, holy; Memorial Acclamation; Great Amen; Lamb of God). The sung text of these should be the same as, or close to, the words prescribed. Although there is a role for a choir at Mass, the congregation must be allowed and encouraged to sing.

6. At the Opening Prayer (Collect), there should be a short but definite silence after 'Let us pray'.

7. Readers should be intelligent, prepared, audible, able to make eye contact. There should be sufficient numbers to allow variety. In particular, different readers should be used when there are two readings before the gospel. Some practice is necessary (including practice in moving to and from the lectern). The proper books should be used, not missalettes. Parishes should also ask: is there a courteous and effective system for dealing with poor or inadequate readers?

8. The psalm should be sung, if possible. Some variation from the prescribed psalm is allowed, as also are metrical versions (but not a non-psalm hymn).

9. General Intercessions: the items are *intentions* for which we are asked to pray, not the prayers themselves. Hence, after each intention and before the invitation for a communal response, there should be a short but definite pause for individual, silent prayer.

How many intentions should there be? Four or five are enough.

How long? Quite short; they are intentions, not prayers or disguised sermons.

They should include topical important concerns, either local or more general.

10. The eucharistic prayer begins with the dialogue before the preface. The 'preface' is part of the eucharistic prayer.

11. There are other eucharistic prayers in addition to nos. 2 and 3.

12. During the doxology at the conclusion of the eucharistic prayer, the consecrated bread and wine are raised in a gesture of offering them to the Father, not of showing them to the people.

13. The greeting of peace should not be prolonged unduly or involve a lot of movement or chatter.

14. 'Blessed are those...' before communion. The Eucharist is a pledge and foretaste of heaven which, in the Apocalypse, is described as a banquet. The liturgy takes up the eschatological theme (e.g., the memorial acclamations; 'as we await the blessed hope...'; the 'Lamb of God' and 'Blessed are those called to the banquet of the Lamb'). The 'banquet' or 'supper' is eschatological, not 'this Mass'.

15. The hosts should be those consecrated at the Mass being celebrated. This is not entirely achievable but the tabernacle should not contain full ciboria 'ready for the Sunday Masses'.

16. Holy communion from the chalice should be offered to all, and this for a number of reasons, not least because the Mass is a renewal of God's covenant with us, expressed in the words '...of my blood of the new and eternal covenant'. Communion from the chalice allows the communicants to partake of this blood of the covenant.

17. A sacred silence should be observed after holy communion. If it is, there is no need to pause after 'Let us pray' before the Prayer after Communion.

18. Dismissal. 'Go forth in peace' better expresses the mission that we receive.

19. Hymns at Mass are often given undue importance. Suitable hymns can be sung at appropriate moments but sometimes silence is preferable. Hymns should have some relation to the liturgy of the day and should not take so much time that they unduly delay the liturgical action.

A recessional hymn should not always be necessary; an organ voluntary can be substituted. Remember that the people have already been told to leave.

20. Eucharistic devotion outside Mass should be fostered by:
- reverence in church;
- genuflections done properly;
- private visits (if it is safe to have the church open);
- services of Benediction and/or holy hour, if and when possible.

PART THREE. THE EUCHARIST: A MYSTERY TO BE LIVED

"If anyone eats of this bread, he will live for ever... He who eats me will live because of me' (John 6:51.56). These words of Jesus, says Pope Benedict, 'make us realise how the mystery 'believed' and 'celebrated' contains an innate power, making it the principle of new life within us'. By receiving the Eucharist, 'we become sharers in the divine life in an ever more adult and conscious way' (§70).

Our eucharistic worship includes and transfigures many aspects of life. We are called to worship God in all the thoughts, words and actions of our lives. Christ (whose whole human life consists in the worship of God) has assured us that 'he who eats me will live because of me'. Pope Benedict is thus able to declare:

The worship of God in our lives cannot be relegated to something private and individual, but tends by its nature to permeate every aspect of our existence. Worship pleasing to God thus becomes a new way of living our whole life, each particular moment of which is lifted up since it is lived as part of a relationship with Christ and as an offering to God. (§70)

The Lord's Day

'From the beginning Christians were clearly conscious of this radical newness which the Eucharist brings to human life' (§72). Sometimes in the early Church this truth was called 'living in accordance with the Lord's Day' because Sunday was the day on which the Christian community gathered in faith to celebrate the Eucharist. The idea of 'living in accordance with the Lord's Day' is still true in our time and it gives added meaning and importance to the obligation of taking part in Sunday Mass. Fulfilment of this obligation enables us to live each day in accordance with what we celebrate on the Lord's Day.

Sunday should also be a day of rest from work. If civil society recognises this, it gives a freedom to people who might otherwise be enslaved by the work they have to do; 'work is for man, not man for work'. Work must be organised with respect for human dignity and must serve the common good.

If a Christian community cannot have Mass on a Sunday because a priest cannot be there, the people should, if possible, go to a place where there is Mass. If this is not reasonably possible, a Liturgy of the Word should take place. This should be carefully and correctly carried out; if holy communion is given, it should be distributed only by someone authorised by the local bishop; and in all such cases the difference between such a liturgy and the celebration of Mass must be clear and understood. Indeed, such assemblies should demonstrate the indispensable ministry of priests and the need to pray to God to send holy priests.

The Apostolic Exhortation urges priests to be willing to visit communities that have no resident priest and to ensure that none 'remain too long without the sacrament of love' (§75).

Taking part in Mass on Sundays and receiving the Body and Blood of Christ, we rediscover the communal dimension of our lives. This communion is twofold: communion with God, Father, Son and Spirit; and communion with our brothers and sisters. If one of these two is missing, so is the other. The secularisation so prevalent in today's world encourages individualism but, as Christians, we are aware that our lives are eucharistic, ecclesial and communitarian. Celebrating the Eucharist makes us belong to a community, Christ's Body, the Church, experienced through our membership of the diocese and the parish.

For everyone in the Church

Eucharistic spirituality is not restricted to Mass and devotion to the Blessed Sacrament. It embraces and affects the whole of our lives, the way that we think and act. Otherwise, our faith would be relegated to the margins and lack relevance for 'ordinary daily life'. Jesus is not a private conviction or an abstract idea.

On the evangelisation of the different cultures in the world, the Exhortation declares that Jesus Christ and the outpouring of the Holy Spirit are capable of 'engaging every cultural reality and bringing to it the leaven of the gospel. It follows that we must be committed to promoting the evangelisation of cultures'. The document adds that 'the Eucharist becomes a criterion for our evaluation of everything that Christianity encounters in different cultures' (§78).

Continuing his consideration of the Eucharist as a mystery to be lived, Pope Benedict writes of how the Eucharist ought to affect the daily lives of lay people, of priests and of consecrated persons.

With regard to the lay faithful, he states that

> the eucharistic sacrifice nourishes and increases within us all that we have already received at baptism, with its call to holiness... The Christian laity, by virtue of their baptism and confirmation and strengthened by the Eucharist, are called to live out the radical newness brought by Christ wherever they find themselves. (§79)

> The eucharistic form of the Christian life is seen in a very
> special way in the priesthood. Priestly spirituality is intrinsi-
> cally eucharistic... [The priest] should make the spiritual life
> his highest priority... To this end, I join the Synod Fathers
> in recommending the daily celebration of Mass, even when
> the faithful are not present. (§80)

Consecrated men and women, though providing many educational and caring services, have, as the principal purpose of their
lives, contemplation and constant union with God in prayer. Such
people will 'find in the celebration of the Eucharist and in eucharistic
adoration the strength necessary for the radical following of Christ,
obedient, poor and chaste' (§81). In particular, consecrated virginity
is related in several ways to the Eucharist. It nourishes and strengthens the vow of virginity which, in its turn, is a sign of the Church's
exclusive devotion to Christ her bridegroom, a sign of God's love for
humanity and a sign, also, of 'the wedding feast of the Lamb', the
goal of all salvation history.

The Eucharist and Our Way of Life

The document goes on to explain how the Eucharist, believed,
celebrated and lived, can produce a moral transformation in us. In
the Eucharist we partake of Christ's self-giving love and are equipped
and committed to live the same charity in thought and deed.

> A Eucharist which does not pass over into the same concrete
> practice of love is intrinsically fragmented... The moral
> transformation implicit in the new worship instituted by
> Christ is a heartfelt yearning to respond to the Lord's love
> with one's whole being. (§82)

Pope Benedict concludes his reflections on the eucharistic form of
the Christian life by emphasising, particularly to those in public life,
that genuine worship can never be only a private matter; it demands
a public witness to our faith. Consequently, 'eucharistic consistency'
(as the Pope calls it) demands that Catholic politicians and legisla-

tors are bound, 'on the basis of a properly formed conscience, to introduce and support laws inspired by values grounded in human nature' (§83). The Pope instances some of these values: respect for life, the family (built on marriage between a man and a woman), freedom to educate one's children.

A mystery to be proclaimed and offered to the world

There are two short appendices to Part Three of the Apostolic Exhortation: *The Eucharist, a mystery to be proclaimed*; and *The Eucharist, a mystery to be offered to the world.*

• A mystery to be proclaimed

In the first of the two we read:

> The love that we celebrate in the sacrament is not something we can keep to ourselves. By its very nature it deserves to be shared with all. What the world needs is God's love; it needs to encounter Christ and believe in him. (§84)

We carry out this mission by the witness of our lives, 'through our actions, words and way of being' (§85). The supreme witness to God's love in Christ is found in the martyrs of the early Church and also of today. Concerned for, and in solidarity with, Christians who live in places where religious freedom is denied them,

> let us pray, therefore, for greater religious freedom in every nation so that Christians, as well the followers of other religions, can freely express their convictions, both as individuals and as communities. (§87)

• A mystery to be offered to the world

In the second appendix to Part Three, Pope Benedict quotes Christ's words: 'The bread I will give is my flesh for the life of the world' (John 6:51) and reminds us of God's saving will for all people. Echoing Pope John Paul's teaching in *Mane Nobiscum Domine* (§28), *Sacramentum Caritatis* insists that our eucharistic faith and worship compel us 'to work for the building of a more just and fraternal world' (§88).

'The relationship between the eucharistic mystery and social commitment must be made explicit' (§89). Pope Benedict develops this statement by declaring that, since Jesus died for all, our participation in the Eucharist demands that we recognise our duty to show our union not only with those who celebrate the Eucharist with us but with all our fellow human beings. We must work for peace and justice, for reconciliation and forgiveness. Participating in the Eucharist, we have to be committed to peacemaking 'in a world scarred by violence and war and, today in particular, by terrorism, economic corruption and sexual exploitation' (§89). Displaced persons and refugees are still numbered in millions; their poverty and degrading living conditions, as well as the plight of all who suffer extreme poverty, are an affront and an accusation which we cannot calmly accept. We must denounce the causes of such suffering, such inhumane situations of injustice and exploitation. The Catholic Church already has a number of appropriate agencies and institutions, notably 'Caritas'. All of us, indeed, are called to 'work tirelessly in the service of the civilisation of love' (§90).

To enable us to be properly prepared for our efforts to end, or at least reduce, the scandalous situations to which so many human beings are condemned, dioceses should try to promote and raise awareness of the Church's social teaching (§91).

Eucharistic spirituality requires that,

> in giving thanks to God through the Eucharist, [we] should be conscious that [we] do so in the name of all creation, aspiring to the sanctification of the world. (§92)

Various allusions in the Mass, for example in the blessing prayers over the bread and wine, illustrate the point: 'this bread...fruit of the earth', 'fruit of the vine', 'the work of human hands' (§92).

Speaking of threats to the environment and our responsibility to protect God's creation. Pope Benedict asserts:

The world is not something indifferent, raw material to be utilised simply as we see fit. Rather, it is part of God's good plan in which all of us are called to be sons and daughters in the one Son of God, Jesus Christ. (§92)

Finally, the Pope promises a new Eucharistic Compendium for the correct understanding, celebration and adoration of the Sacrament of the Altar, to help us 'to believe, celebrate and live ever more fully the mystery of the Eucharist' (§93).

CONCLUSION

There is a short epilogue to *Sacramentum Caritatis*. 'Dear brothers and sisters,' Pope Benedict writes, 'the Eucharist is at the root of every form of holiness and each of us is called to the fullness of life in the Holy Spirit... The celebration and worship of the Eucharist enables us to draw near to God's love and to persevere in that love' (§94). The Pope insistently asks that we 'spare no effort in promoting an authentically eucharistic Christian spirituality' which will lead us closer to God, Father, Son and Spirit, for our personal and communal sanctification and bring us into solidarity with all men and women, for whom Jesus gave his life.

Pope Benedict asks us to seek the prayers of all the holy men and women down through the ages whose lives have been characterised by love of the Eucharist; in a special way he reminds us of those who suffered martyrdom because of their love of, and need for, the Mass. Above all, we pray to Mary, 'finest icon' of the Church, 'singular model of the eucharistic life', who conceived and gave birth to him who is truly present in the Eucharist (§96).

The Apostolic Exhortation ends with these beautiful and inspiring words:

Through the intercession of the Blessed Virgin Mary, may the Holy Spirit kindle within us the same ardour experienced by the disciples on the way to Emmaus and renew our 'eucharistic wonder' through the splendour and beauty radiating from the liturgical rite, the efficacious sign of the infinite beauty of the holy mystery of God. Those disciples arose and returned in haste to Jerusalem in order to share their joy with their brothers and sisters in the faith. True joy is found in recognising that the Lord is still with us, our faithful companion along the way. The Eucharist makes us discover that Christ, risen from the dead, is our contemporary in the mystery of the Church, his body. Of this mystery of love we have become witnesses. Let us encourage one another to walk joyfully, our hearts filled with wonder, towards our encounter with the Holy Eucharist, so that we may experience and proclaim to others the truth of the words with which Jesus took leave of the disciples: 'Lo, I am with you always, until the end of the world'. (§97)

A Comment

In the Apostolic Constitution, Pope Benedict has based his teaching very much on the Propositions formulated by the Synod of Bishops of 2005 and offered to him to use as he saw fit in his post-synodal document. The Pope chooses a threefold exposition of the Eucharist: a mystery to be believed, celebrated, lived. The second of these three parts is mainly practical, urging a worthy celebration of Mass and especially one that fosters full, active and prayerful involvement of those taking part, each according to his or her proper role.

The first and third parts of *Sacramentum Caritatis* open up a rich spirituality of the Eucharist. There are paragraphs in which the Pope's thoughts and insights are so profound and dense as to require an understanding that is indeed demanding. However, the Apostolic Exhortation repays all the efforts we have to make to follow the Pope's line of thought and so be enriched with a fresh appreciation of the wonderful gift that is the Eucharist.

The Eucharist is not just an important element in our spirituality;

it totally permeates it, almost like the soul in the body. All of our spirituality has to be eucharistic, not only in its foundation but as an essential constituent of its very being.

Pope Benedict's repeated insistence that, for us all, spirituality is fundamentally and essentially eucharistic is a truth that should enable us to have a new and greater attachment to the Eucharist. More than that, it offers us the opportunity to grow in love for Christ our Lord, for the Blessed Trinity which he makes present to us, for Mary and the saints, and for all men and women for whom Jesus offered his life as our Saviour.

> Sacred Banquet of the Eucharist,
> in which Christ is consumed
> and his passion made present.
> Our minds are filled with gratitude
> and a pledge of future glory is granted us.

13th century, attributed to St Thomas Aquinas. The original version is on p.21.